# MEMORIES OF A GAME RANGER

# MEMORIES OF A GAME RANGER

Harry Wolhuter

Illustrations by C.T. Astley-Maberly

Protea Book House
Pretoria
2019

A portion of the proceeds from sales will be going to WESSA
(the Wildlife and Environmental Society of South Africa)
to assist the Conservation Division.

*Memories of a game ranger* – Harry Wolhuter
First edition, first impression in 1948 by The Wildlife Protection and
Conservation Society of South Africa
10th impression 1970
Second edition, first impression in 1971 by Fontana Books
Third edition, first impression in 2008 by Protea Book House
Third edition, second impression 2010
Third edition, third impression 2013
Third edition, fourth impression 2019

PO Box 35110, Menlo Park, 0102
1067 Burnett Street, Hatfield, Pretoria
8 Minni Street, Clydesdale, Pretoria
protea@intekom.co.za
www.proteaboekhuis.com

Cover design: Etienne van Duyker
Front cover image: Getty/Gallo Images
Typography: 12 on 15 pt Joanna MT by Etienne van Duyker

Printed by **novus print**, a Novus Holdings company

© 2008, 2010, 2013, 2019 Protea Book House
ISBN 978-1-86919-360-7

All rights reserved. No part of this book may be reproduced or
transmitted in any form or by any electronic or mechanical means,
including photocopying and recording, or by any other
information storage or retrieval system, without
written permission from the publisher.

# CONTENTS

Preface  9

Foreword  11

Chapter 1  Early years  15

Chapter 2  In the Lowveld  29

Chapter 3  Steinacker's Horse  49

Chapter 4  Wartime adventures  62

Chapter 5  Sabi Game Reserve  84

Chapter 6  Attacked by lions  96

Chapter 7  A ranger's life  113

Chapter 8  Man's best friend  130

Chapter 9  Poachers  148

Chapter 10  Notes on animal life  163

Chapter 11  Wild pets  184

Chapter 12  Unwelcome encounters  202

Chapter 13  Snakes  220

Chapter 14  Rainmakers  231

Chapter 15  Native reserve  247

Chapter 16  Birds  264

Chapter 17  Horses  272

Chapter 18  Lions  280

Postscript  291

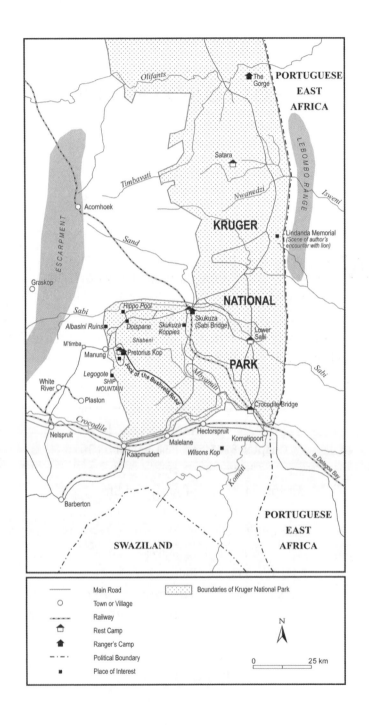

# EDITOR'S NOTE

When Harry Wolhuter wrote *Memories of a game ranger*, the term "natives" was not thought to be derogatory. This usage has not been changed in this edition – it is not our intention to give offence, but to protect the work's authenticity.

The original measurements and place names have also been retained, but a metric table appears on p. 292 and the old and new place names appear on p. 293.

The Author.

# PREFACE

Since my retirement on completion of forty-four years' service as a ranger in the Kruger National Park, a number of my friends have suggested that I ought to record in book form some of the experiences of a life which in many ways has been an unusual one, and to me at least full of interest.

After considerable hesitation I eventually yielded to persuasion, and the following pages are the result. They deal mainly with a world very different from that of today, for the changes which have taken place in Lowveld life and conditions exceed those which have occurred anywhere else in South Africa. What, only forty years ago, was a wild, trackless and almost unknown country, has now, thanks to the attraction of the Kruger National Park, become a popular resort for visitors not only from every part of South Africa, but from overseas as well.

I felt, however, that my rather promiscuous notes required expert editing, and I am doubly grateful to Mr C.T. Astley-Maberley not only for having so ably performed this task, but for having illustrated the book. Few other professional artists are so well acquainted with wildlife or have spent so much time in delineating it in its natural surroundings; in fact, in the early days of the Park he was accustomed to wander about alone on a bicycle sketching such animals as he met; a feat which would not be permitted nowadays!

My sincere thanks are due to Mrs Stevenson-Hamilton for the silhouette on the title page of this book, and to Mr A. Orme of Johannesburg, who designed the dust cover and also rendered very material help in arranging the blocks.

My best thanks are also due to Mr B.A. Key of the Wild Life Protection Society for having so kindly undertaken all the publication arrangements, as well as for the early encouragement which he gave me towards undertaking the task of committing my memories to paper. Whatever ultimate success the book may have is due, in the first place, to his untiring efforts and zeal towards ensuring that it be produced in the most attractive and decorative way possible.

H.C. Wolhuter
Pretorius Kop
June 1948

# FOREWORD

When, in July 1902, I made my debut in the Lowveld as warden of the newly proclaimed Sabi Game Reserve, I naturally looked round anxiously for someone of local experience who might serve me as guide, philosopher and friend.

Every "old hand" whom I approached said the same thing, "Try and get hold of Harry Wolhuter; he knows the country better than anyone else: give him a horse, a rifle and a pair of saddlebags and he will start off for anywhere at five minutes' notice!"

When at last, through the good offices of my friend Major Greenhill-Gardyne, then Adjutant of Steinacker's Horse, I was successful in making contact with him, I found that Wolhuter's appearance and manner justified his reputation. Tall, spare but powerfully built; purposeful, for all his quiet voice and unassuming manner, he seemed emblematical of the best type of pioneer hunter.

It did not take long to bring home to me how fortunate I was to have found such an assistant so soon, and in all the years of close companionship and friendship that have since passed, I have never ceased to regard the day of that first meeting as a red letter one in my life.

I suppose there can be few if any men in all Africa possessing a deeper knowledge and wider experience of bush lore in all its phases, and in his prime he held all the qualities requisite to give effect to that knowledge and experience: a powerful frame, an iron constitution, cool courage and quiet determination. In addition, his complete mastery of the local Bantu language, and acquaintance with their customs, earned him exceptional liking and respect among the tribal natives.

His unique exploit in killing, single-handed and armed only with a knife, a full-grown male lion which had seized and was carrying him off, was in itself a feat rendering superfluous any further tributes to his rare courage and coolness; but it is worth remarking that in the many hazards – happily all safely surmounted – which he has since incurred in the course of his duties, his nerve has shown itself to be just as calm and steady as it was when he underwent that terrible experience.

Unfortunately he never fully got over the injuries he then received. The long time which had to elapse before his highly septic wounds could be treated would undoubtedly have proved fatal to anyone with a less sound constitution, or, at the moment, less hard and fit. As it was, though he did not, as was for some time feared, lose his right arm, yet some after-effects persisted, which, added to the results of constant attacks of malaria, including two of the usually fatal blackwater fever, have ever since affected his health in various ways.

Nevertheless, right up to the date of his retirement in 1946 he was still taking chances with lions, and only a year or two before had even dispatched a badly injured one with a knife, "to save a cartridge"!

Mr Astley-Maberley, who has undertaken the task of putting the original notes into book form, has wisely kept almost throughout to the author's own words and phrases.

I may add that the records of natural phenomena of various

kinds may be taken as strictly accurate, as coming from an exceptionally careful and experienced observer.

In respect of personal performance, there appears no doubt a certain reticence and tendency to understatement which are natural to Harry Wolhuter, and are very attractive traits in his character; he avoids personal credit when possible, and it was only after considerable difficulty that his friends induced him to put his various adventures on paper.

I esteem it as the highest privilege to have been asked to write a foreword to my old friend's memoirs.

J. Stevenson-Hamilton, Late Warden,
*Kruger National Park*

CHAPTER 1
==========

# EARLY YEARS

I was born in the town of Beaufort West in the Karoo on 14 February 1877, and my childhood recollections are those of a pleasant, carefree life. They say that "the child is father to the man", and certainly in my case I was always fond of hunting and life in the veld. Although my adult life's work has been employed almost entirely in the guardianship and protection of wildlife, during my very early years I was, as I fancy is the case with most children (at any rate in those days in the sunny veld of South Africa), concerned more with perfecting my skill to outwit and destroy it! From using a catapult I graduated to an air gun, and finally matriculated with a muzzle-loader that could fire both shot and bullets.

We used to go shooting on Saturdays, but game was already scarce in those parts and it was a long time before I shot my first buck. We were not allowed much pocket money so we had to make our own gunpowder, which was naturally very crude stuff that exploded with a deafening roar. The old barrel must have been made of very good steel otherwise it

would almost certainly have burst.

'We were accustomed to mould our own bullets from any old bits of lead we could acquire, and in addition to these we used the covering of tea chests, which was made of lead in those days. So far as caps were concerned, we simply used the same old ones over and over again – taking the head of a match and inserting it inside the cap. Sometimes it worked and sometimes it did not.

One day, try as we would, the cap would not go off, so we brought it home and, taking it out, tried to open the nipple with a pin. While fiddling about with the pin in the nipple hole I somehow ignited a bit of the head of the match and with a fearful bang off went the shot – just missing one of my brothers who was sitting beside me by about an inch! That proved to be a good lesson for me, as from that day I was scared of loading firearms and indeed have since then seen several accidents of that sort caused through carelessness. On top of that I also received a tremendous thrashing from my father.

I was never keen on lessons and going to school, and I very often used to play truant and take the old gun with me. On one occasion, upon refusing to go to school, my father had me loaded on and tied to a wheelbarrow and he then ordered the old gardener to trundle me to school. Being naturally disinclined for school work I was often kept in after hours, and I was often locked in the schoolroom to do overtime with my lessons.

I remember one afternoon, on one of these occasions when I had been kept in, instead of attending to my work I roamed round the school from which there was a door leading to the storeroom in which the mistress kept her stores. While foraging round I found a large earthenware jar which, in those days, was often bought already filled with ginger. It had a very small top in which I could only just insert my fingers, but I found it to be full of beautiful tomato jam! The following day, of course, I was again kept in, but this time I came prepared with a spoon. Very little of the tomato jam remained when I had finished, but unfortunately I must have left a trace of it on the shelf, and once again I received a good thrashing. After this that door was always kept locked.

When I reached the age when most boys think they would like to sample tobacco, I invested in a pipe; but having been warned by my father that I must not smoke until I was twenty years old, it had to be kept a secret. Then I thought I would like to chew tobacco in imitation of some other boys about my own age. One day when I had a good big plug of strong Boer tobacco in my cheek, I suddenly came face to face with my father, who remarked, "What is the matter with your face; you look as though you have a gumboil! Let me have a look at it." There was only one way to avoid a thrashing, so I swallowed the plug and replied that I was all right and had not got any gumboil. So he let me go, but five minutes later I was violently sick.

Another day I was quietly smoking my pipe round a corner when the old man suddenly came on me. I hastily shoved the pipe into my pocket, but unfortunately the loose and dry Boer

tobacco spilled out of the bowl and set fire to the lining of my pocket. My father exclaimed, "You seem to be on fire; turn out your pockets!" Of course when I did so out came the pipe, which meant a thrashing, and on top of it a threat to lock me in my room with a pipe, a box of matches and a yard length of plug tobacco, and to keep me there until I had smoked it all. Now, I liked an occasional pipe, but was far from relishing the idea of having to smoke a yard of strong Boer tobacco at one go. So after this I decided to keep my pipe and tobacco in the bush and to go and have a draw when I happened to feel inclined.

During the summer holidays we used to spend the whole day swimming and boating in the dam, then the biggest (as it may still be) in the Karoo. We made our own boats; fashioning them out of ordinary boxes with a V-shaped front and back. These boats would only hold one of us at a time, and as we were accustomed to paddle ourselves through a mile of water in them it is really a wonder that none of us drowned. Actually the boats very often capsized; but as we wore no clothes on these excursions and were all good swimmers, we always managed to gain shore.

When I was about thirteen years old my parents decided to come to the Transvaal. At that time the railway was completed only as far as Kimberley and so from there we trekked by mule wagon to Johannesburg, where I remained when my people went on.

At about fourteen I found my first job, at a trading store at Maraisburg. My salary was three pounds a month and my employer never neglected to tell me that I was not worth it. In addition to the usual trading business, this store also ran a post office.

After a while my employer sold the business, as he wanted to go to Johannesburg, and as I had nothing better in view at the time I accepted his proposal for me to accompany him. On the day we left Maraisburg I was instructed to hand over the mail to the new postmaster. He had arrived by Zeederberg's coach, as the rail had not yet been constructed from Krugersdorp to Johannesburg and all passengers and mail arrived by coach.

I remember, incidentally, that Zeederberg's coach had some very good horses, and the bugle always sounded as the coach came in. On this occasion the coach only remained for about half an hour at the hotel (which was next door), just long enough to allow the passengers time for refreshment. During this half hour I had to hand over the post office, instruct the new man how to make up the post, collect my belongings and reach the coach in time before it left again.

Now in those days the Mining Commissioner's office was in Florida; and as there was no post office there, all the post for Florida had to come to Maraisburg. The revenue collected by the Mining Commissioner's office was also sent to the Maraisburg office by registered parcel, amounting sometimes to over a thousand pounds. On the previous day such a parcel had been handed to me for registration, and as there was no safe in the post office I had put it on the shelf at the back of the counter. I now showed it to the new postmaster and told him to include it in the bag, seal it and hand it to the driver of the coach, from whom he was to obtain a receipt for it.

I then caught the coach and departed for Johannesburg, where I found a job in a bar and billiard room.

After about five days a policeman arrived and enquired whether I was Harry Wolhuter. Upon my replying in the affirmative he proceeded to arrest me for theft! To my considerable alarm he informed me that the registered parcel that had previously been handed to me from the Mining Commissioner's office at Florida had not arrived at the Johannesburg Post Office; that I was responsible for it; and that I had to accompany him to Maraisburg. He had with him a cart and horses, and off we went. When we reached Maraisburg we went straight to the corner of the shop which was the post office and there, on the shelf where I had originally left it, lay the registered parcel. The new postmaster had neglected to include it in the post bag; and since it was said to contain £800, my relief at its safe recovery may be imagined!

The Bar and Billiard Room in which I now worked was known as the Black Cat. Such places in those days were frequented by all kinds of odd and reckless characters, and among the regular patrons of the old Black Cat were individuals picturesquely known in the vernacular as *Boer verneukers* (farmer cheaters).

Their principal method of obtaining a living was as follows: They would sally forth along the main roads leading to Johannesburg, some on horseback and some in Cape carts, until they met a farmer coming in with his produce. The farmer would then be engaged in conversation, and he would presently be offered a price for his whole load; these worthies of course being well acquainted with prevailing market prices. The poor old farmer, as a rule, was ignorant of current prices in town, or else, perhaps, it was his first load; at any rate, not knowing better, he would usually willingly accept this seemingly providential offer, and the *Boer verneukers* would pay him so much on account – the balance to come when he had arrived with his wagon on the market square. The successful businessmen would then return and hand over the load to the Market Master, and of course reap a handsome profit from the proceeds. Judging by the amount of money these men spent in the bar they apparently found it a most profitable business.

During my spare time at the Black Cat I had plenty of opportunities for practising all the different shots that I had seen the crack players use, and I very soon became a good billiard player. In fact, although still a youngster, I could hold my own with anyone.

After leaving that job I did not have a chance of handling a billiard cue again for many years. The next time I tried was in the hotel at Pietersburg and I found then that I had forgotten everything I knew, and after I had nearly torn a hole in the billiard table cloth I had to give it up!

In due course I wearied of life in Johannesburg, and feeling the call of the veld becoming ever more insistent I decided to join my parents at Legogote in the Eastern Transvaal. My mother, in any case, had repeatedly begged me to join the family circle once more, and my father had established a trading store, so that there seemed to be every encouragement for me to go. Before dismissing the Black Cat period in my life altogether, however, I must relate one incident that serves to indicate the sort of conditions under which I then lived.

The Black Cat Bar was established, in those days, in the Market Square. The room I occupied was in the backyard and as it had no window I was in the habit of leaving the door open on hot nights. I used to hang my clothes over the chair at the foot of my bed. One night a thief entered the room and stole all my clothes; and since these comprised everything I then possessed, I had no option but to remain in bed until my employer came to enquire why I was not up. In fact, I had to remain in bed until he managed to get me some other clothes.

In order to reach the Eastern Transvaal I had to interview a "forwarding agent" to see whether I could contact a wagon leaving for Barberton, as all goods going to that place had to proceed by ox wagon; the railway not having yet been constructed. I was completely without funds. My employer at the Black Cat never paid me, so I had to accept any conditions that were offered in the way of transport, and the best the agent could offer was to place me on the waiting list for something to turn up. However, in a few days he informed me that a wagon loading for Barberton would be along on the following day, and in due course I interviewed its owner.

This gentleman said that, since I was unable to pay for my passage, he would agree to take me along with him provided I would assist him with the herding of the oxen, cook his food, take the tow rope (the leading "riem" attached to the heads of the two front oxen so that the team could be led where necessary) and do all the other odd jobs, as he was quite alone with the wagon. Of course I was only too glad to accept these conditions in return for the lift, and I commenced my new duties on that same day.

My bedding was very simple: it consisted of just one blanket (no mattress or pillow), in which I used to curl myself, head and all, underneath the wagon when bedtime came; but nonetheless I slept well, in spite of the hard ground, as I was always very tired

by the end of the day. The nights were extremely cold, it being the middle of July – the height of the South African winter.

My new boss used to awaken me before daylight to loosen the oxen from the trek-tows to which they had been tied during the night, and to take them out to graze before the daily trek. I well remember how bitterly cold those early mornings usually were, the "riems" with which the oxen were tied being often frozen so stiff that it proved a difficult and painful task untying them with my benumbed fingers, while all around the ground lay covered with hard white frost.

When my boss considered it to be time to inspan he would crack his whip, and on hearing this I would drive in the oxen and we would inspan and trek. When the road was good I used to ride on the wagon, which I enjoyed thoroughly. He had two very good front oxen that could follow the road without a leader, but when the road was bad, and when crossing spruits, I had to jump off the wagon and lead them.

One of the front oxen I remember well: his name was Erland and sometimes he became bad-tempered and poked viciously with his horns, and I had to keep well out of reach of the swing-

ing head. However, in spite of the hardships and the paucity of the fare, I really enjoyed the trip. I was travelling through new country and seeing new sights day after day, and the spirits of youth are wonderfully buoyant.

One evening we caught up with some other wagons also on their way to Barberton with transport. After we had tied up the oxen and made everything snug for the night, we strolled over to visit the men and I noticed at once that they were the worse for liquor. In fact they seemed to be well equipped with brandy, which they generously offered to my boss and also to myself. I had never tasted spirits before, not even when I was barman in the old Black Cat in Johannesburg, where I had never drunk anything stronger than lemonade; and I quickly spat out the brandy, wondering to myself how men could drink such stuff. In after years, however, I discovered that, in moderation at any rate, it had its virtues!

After we had spent a convivial evening and returned to our own wagon, I asked my master where our friends had collected all this brandy. He told me that they had two wagonloads of brandy which they had loaded at Eerstefabriek, near Pretoria. This brandy was known as Nelmapius, after the person who had the sole concession for distilling it. I enquired how they could extract the liquor from the barrels without it being noticed. "Oh," he said, "they drill a small hole with a gimlet into the barrel, tap it into a dish, and then plug the hole in the barrel with a wooden peg, similar in colour to the barrel. In this way the tampering escapes notice, and any apparent discrepancy in weight when the barrel is offloaded in Barberton is always put down to evaporation!"

In due course we reached Kaapsche Hoop, and here we met some trek-boers who were trekking down to the winter veld with their sheep and cattle. They told me that they were coming down to camp on the Sigaas River (which is now in the Kruger National Park) and that they had to pass right in front of my father's place. This seemed to be too good an opportunity for me to lose and I was delighted when they consented to my accompanying them on condition that I helped to drive the sheep.

And so I now became a shepherd! I cannot say that I enjoyed this new job very much, as some of the sheep were always lagging behind. At the Crocodile River there was, of course, no bridge in those days, and I well remember how we had to construct one to enable the sheep to cross by placing the wagons one after another, back to front, across the river.

Eventually we reached Legogote and thus the end of my journey, and I need hardly say how pleased my people were to see me home again, and I to see them, and it was with a very happy heart that I bade farewell to my kind friends, who continued their way to the winter veld.

I now settled down in my home and there led a very pleasant life, as there was plenty of game in the vicinity. So our free moments were well occupied, though my father made my two brothers and myself work very hard on the farm during the week. Saturday afternoons and Sundays, however, were ours to go

hunting – which, I need hardly add, was our favourite form of amusement. On moonlight nights, too, we used to take the dogs and hunt porcupines, springhares and anything else the dogs could catch.

I can see some of my game-preserving friends shake their heads sadly at this barbarous preoccupation on the part of a future game ranger! But boys will be boys. And after all, it was a first-rate training in veld life. We hunted over much of the ground that is now within the boundaries of the Kruger National Park – sometimes in company with the trek-boers and sometimes on our own account. Game, however, was not as plentiful there as it is now.

As there were no educational facilities in the district then, my parents went to Belfast in order that the younger children could attend school, while I remained on at Legogote to look after the farm and trading store. In due course I built up quite a nice herd of cattle, all of which were doomed to be lost when the rinderpest swept through the country in 1896–97.

At that time there were no bridges across the large rivers such as the White, Nels and Crocodile; so during the rainy season one was often completely cut off for months since it very frequently rained for weeks at a time. It was a common experience to lack provisions and I remember on one occasion being unable to obtain any for three months; the only food available being green mealies, which form a most popular South African dish. However, when one has had to face it three times a day, with no variety, for several months on end, its attractions are apt to pall; with the result that I have been unable ever since to look at a green mealie!

## Chapter 2

# IN THE LOWVELD

Legogote, near which my father's store was established, is the native name of a curious, projecting peak that forms a well-known and conspicuous landmark near the western boundary of the present Kruger National Park. It can easily be seen from Pretorius Kop, and the main road from White River to the Park passes it closely. I think its name means "klipspringer", as the native name for that attractive small rock-dwelling antelope is *legoka*. There used to be a great many klipspringers inhabiting the koppie.

During the time I was living there the Native Commissioner for the whole of the low country was Abel Erasmus. I have never known natives to fear and respect any white man as they did him. If a native gave trouble all one had to do was to threaten to report him to "Habel" or "Madabula" (the latter being his

native name – "the man who shoots"), and that was sufficient for the trouble to cease forthwith. I am aware that he was often blamed for ill-treating natives, but in reality this was unjust; all cases of deliberate ill-treatment having been perpetrated by his subordinates and his head policemen, without his knowledge.

His head policeman, Tobais Mlamba, grew up in Erasmus' household. His father was a headman of the Mambai tribe, which inhabited a great part of the Lowveld. Tobais claimed that he was of royal blood and built himself a kraal called Mtomene near the Sigaas River, which is now in the native reserve. He obtained his wives from the king's kraal in Swaziland and, since they were of high estate, he had to pay big lobola – from thirty to forty head of cattle – for a wife, but cattle were easily found! All he had to do was to send out his policemen and tell his natives that the chief wanted so many head of cattle with which to buy a wife, and the cattle had to be produced.

He always had very good salted horses and he kept several beautiful greyhounds which also came from the royal kraal. These he used for coursing duiker, steenbok and hares: this was considered the correct thing for chiefs to do in those days, and most of them used to organise hunts at regular periods. Tobais would pay good prices for his greyhounds, was quite well educated and could speak Afrikaans fluently. I often visited his kraal at Mtomene; it was beautifully laid out with the usual cattle kraal in the centre and well-thatched huts surrounding it. His wives, of whom there were many, were all of superior type, being of royal blood.

At one time Tobais intended to grow a lot of wheat, as he had seen the white farmers do at Kruger's Post, Erasmus' farm. To do this, of course, it was necessary for him to irrigate; so he hired a European to take the levels from the Sigaas River to his proposed wheat lands and he employed another to make the water furrow, which would be a few miles long. But, unfortunately for him, then came the Boer War – and that was the end of Tobais. I never saw him again after the war was over, and in reply to my enquiries I was informed that his power was broken and that he was no longer a man of any account.

About this time a serious epidemic of malaria broke out around the area now occupied by the villages of White River and Plaston, and it was thought that the construction of the Netherlands Railway from Delagoa Bay to Pretoria, then in progress, had something to do with it as the workmen employed there were dying every day. Everyone was down with it, no one could go to the help of a neighbour; but when I myself had recovered sufficiently I visited some of the farm houses, gave the occupiers quinine, and otherwise did what I could for them. On coming to the farm house where Plaston is now, I found it shut up, the windows closed and no sign of life except a dog, a few fowls and a couple of pigs. I opened the door and at once noticed the strong, sour smell then associated with malaria, which in those days appeared of a more virulent nature than is the case today.

I found the farmer, a man named Bronkhorst, together with two children lying dead in one bed; in another, alongside, were his wife and two more children, all so ill that they could hardly speak. All I could do at the moment was to give them water to drink, for which they were crying, and I then went to get help from the neighbours. We buried the man and the two dead children, and took the woman and the other two to some relatives of theirs, where they eventually recovered.

I came to another house just in time to see the death of a girl about sixteen, at whose funeral I also assisted. At that period it had not been discovered that mosquitoes were the carriers of malaria, so no precautions were taken against being bitten by the insects.

Among the settlers who came to White River in the early days was a couple with a family of five sons and a daughter. Although they called themselves farmers they never did any cultivation, but lived mainly on game. They kept some oxen and a wagon, used for transporting the family about from place to place. Their wants were few. During the construction of the Netherlands Railway from Lourenço Marques to Pretoria one of the sons who was doing transport work on the construction was returning home (in the neighbourhood of what now is Plaston) for the weekend.

As was the invariable custom, he had his rifle with him – no Boer in those days ever travelled without one – and just after crossing the Crocodile River he saw, soon after sunset, a hippo grazing on the bank, which he shot. He then proceeded home, loaded up the whole family on the wagon, and returned to the place. There they all camped, skinned the hippo, made the hide into sjamboks, the fat into soap, and the meat into biltong. On completion of the task they all re-embarked on the wagon and went home.

Another of the brothers contracted a bad attack of malaria and became delirious. He was rather religious and from his ravings his family thought he must be a prophet. Accordingly all the relatives inspanned their oxen and trekked *en masse* to see Hendrik. In his delirium he prophesied that the end of the world was at hand, and that they must kill and eat all their cattle. They promptly began on Hendrik's, but, after they had killed and eaten six of his fattest oxen, Hendrik recovered and put a stop to it. They all then inspanned and returned to their homes. All these people were extremely religious and knew their Bible from cover to cover, in fact, it was the only book they ever read.

Before my parents left Legogote, when I was about fifteen, a wagon outspanned one day near the farm. That evening I wandered over to the camp and the owner of the wagon suggested I should accompany him on a hunting trip to the Lowveld. Of course, I was delighted at the prospect, but first I had to obtain my parents' consent. At first my mother was rather dubious, as we did not know the man, but eventually (under pressure) she agreed.

The next morning we set out, and I was a happy lad! We did a little shooting on the way and finally we arrived in the area now known as the Satara section of the Kruger National Park, which was then, as now, the best giraffe country. I was given special instructions to the effect that, when we located giraffe, I was not to shoot or even carry a rifle: my duty being to turn the animals and drive them towards the hunter, who, being a heavy man, was unable to ride his horse fast enough to get up to them.

I, on the contrary, being a lightweight, was mounted on his fastest horse, and incidentally was a good rider for my years.

One day we found a troop of giraffe. I immediately galloped after them, and as the country was fairly open succeeded twice in bringing them near enough for him to shoot, but on turning them for the third time I could not locate him. Probably in the excitement of the chase I had lost my bearings, but I still kept galloping after them and trying to turn them.

Presently the giraffes crossed a spruit that was of a very swampy nature, and one of them, a cow, while floundering through a particularly boggy place got held fast in the mud and so was unable to gain the further bank of the spruit. The more she struggled, the deeper she sank, until finally she became quite helpless. I sat on my horse and looked at her for a long time, thinking regretfully how easily I could shoot her if only I had a rifle, and I did not like to leave this giraffe. And then quite suddenly it struck me that I might as well try and cut her throat with my pocketknife! I remember the knife well: it was a "Joseph Rogers" with a staghorn handle.

I rode up to the giraffe. The horse disliked its scent and needed some persuasion on my part, but eventually it seemed to overcome this prejudice and, being lighter in weight than the giraffe, did not sink into the mud. When I had come close enough I took out my pocketknife and slashed away at the poor beast's neck as high as I could reach, and since the animal was of course held fast in the mud it could neither move nor defend itself in any way. I continued to saw away at its neck with its blood splashing all over me, until from sheer loss of blood the huge beast toppled over.

Then, the excitement being over, I was conscious of a sense of regret, and it seemed to me that I had perpetrated a dreadfully cruel and bloodthirsty thing – almost a crime. I must admit that it was indeed a bloodthirsty thing to have done, and yet, on after-thought, I realised that, had I not put it out of its misery by the only means at my disposal, the poor creature would only have died a lingering death in the mud or perhaps it might have been mauled to death by hyenas or other carnivores.

So, after reflecting somewhat sadly at this scene of my first tri-umph at big-game hunting, I rode away to search for the camp. Fortunately, although I was lost, I presently regained my bearings and reached the wagon safely. When asked where I had been and why I had not turned the giraffes a third time, and why I was cov-ered with blood, I related my story. As it must certainly have sounded rather a "tall" one, needless to say I was not at first believed; so I suggested that if the wagon was sent with me we could go and skin the giraffe. This was done, and it proved to be a very fat cow.

During the time I was living at Legogote I often used to see a Zulu by the name of Jan Greik who used to come to my store and buy his requirements. He could speak English fluently, which was quite unique in those days. He told me that he used to work in a butcher's shop in Durban and that was where he learnt to speak English. He had come to this part of the world with transport wagons from Natal. He married a native woman of these parts for whom he paid the usual lobola.

He seemed to have a certain amount of influence over the local natives. One day one of the natives who lived on my farm, called Willeman, with whom I often used to go out hunting as he was about my own age, came to me very mysteriously and told me that very soon, perhaps that night, there was to be a native rising and that all the farmers in the White River area, myself included, were to be killed and all their stock taken. This was indeed very hard to believe, as the natives and the farmers round about seemed to be on very good terms.

Willeman said that he and his four brothers were told to murder me and take my livestock and the stock in the store and that other natives had been likewise detailed to kill the different farmers. I asked him who the instigator of all this was. At first he refused to tell me, but eventually he admitted that it was Jan Greik.

That night I took my rifle and blankets and all the cartridges I had and slept in the veld a short distance from my house, but nothing happened that night or the second night. I then rode over

to Willeman's kraal and accused him of having fooled me, but he told me that the whole rising had fallen flat as some of the natives had refused to carry out Jan Greik's instructions.

There were no police nearer than Barberton in those days and in any case there was nothing to prove that Jan Greik was the instigator of all this.

Some 20 years later while I was spending some of my leave on my farm De Rust, one of the neighbouring farmers arrived at my house to say that the next night, which was the night of Dingaan's Day[1], all the natives in the district were rising and were to kill the white population. He advised me to clear out with all my family and go into laager at White River, and on hearing my refusal to go he seemed very surprised.

Anyway, I thanked him for his information and that night naturally was a sleepless one for me. I had my rifle and 100 rounds of ammunition alongside my bed and I knew that my dogs, which were very good watchdogs, would give the alarm. Again nothing happened, for which I was very thankful. Later I heard that most of the surrounding farmers had packed up all they could on their wagons and trekked into White River. How these reports got around no one seemed to know.

While at Legogote I often visited my nearest neighbour – Bill Sanderson. He had a native trading station and he also farmed cat-

---

[1] December 16, now Day of Reconciliation

tle in quite a big way. He was a Scot and had come to this country as quite a young man, first trying his luck at the alluvial gold diggings around Pilgrim's Rest and Spitzkop which were going on at that time. He had two brothers, Bob and Tom, who were also in the country. Readers of *Jock of the Bushveld* will probably remember the mention of the Sanderson brothers in that wonderful book.

Bill and Bob afterwards bought a farm near Sabie called Ceylon, where they farmed for some years; and when this became too civilised for their liking they came down to the farm Peebles near Legogote. Bob eventually settled on a farm six miles above Klip Koppies.

The Sanderson brothers used to visit the Lowveld regularly every winter on shooting trips, through much of the country now in the Kruger National Park, and they shot all kinds of big game except elephant. Bill was a great lover of dogs and horses. He always had very fine horses which he looked after a great deal better than he looked after himself! He was a magnificent horseman. He always maintained a large pack of dogs with which he was accustomed to hunt bushbuck, duiker and m'zumbi (red duiker) in the kloofs of his farm. He was also a first-class rifle shot.

At one time he tried to breed horses, but as they had to be what was known as "salted" – that is, recovered from horse sickness and thus immunised to that disease – they were hard to obtain and very expensive when one could buy them. Unfortunately his horse breeding was not a success: somehow or other an outbreak of

glanders was contracted among them and they all died, except his own particular riding horse, a beautiful grey gelding called Charles, which he rode till it died of old age.

All his dogs were allowed to enter the dining room at meal times, and the room being moreover infested with flies, the meal was never very appetising – at least so far as visitors were concerned!

Poor old Bill. He finally took sick with some internal complaint and went to Johannesburg for treatment, but those being the days before X-ray, I do not think the doctors really knew what was wrong with him before they operated, and what they then found is unknown as he did not recover.

Bob at one time was a transport rider. He always had two or three wagons on the road, usually between Nelspruit and the gold mines at Sabie and Pilgrim's Rest. He prided himself greatly on his fine team of Afrikander oxen. During the Boer War Bob Sanderson took ill and went to Barberton Hospital, where he died.

As previously mentioned, when rinderpest killed off all my cattle I once again had to set out in search of a job. I obtained one as manager of Mr H.L. Hall's farm near Nelspruit. The farm was then known as Riverside, but now it is called Mattafin.

At that time, all dwellers in the Lowveld suffered greatly from malaria. We were unaware of the true cause of it and consequently we frequently suffered from recurrences as well as new doses. A man would get up in the morning feeling quite fit, but by nine or ten o'clock he would be down with a bad dose of "shakes". We were told that quinine was a preventive, but those were the days before tabloids[2] and the only quinine obtainable was in powder form, which we were accustomed to take a teaspoonful at a time.

---

[2] tablets

How many grains that contained goodness only knows! It kept us going, but we never got rid of the parasites.

I remember once, when returning from a visit to my old friend Bill Sanderson, that though apparently perfectly fit when I left his place, I felt by nine o'clock a dose of malaria coming on. I still had to ride twenty miles to reach home and I rode as hard as I could while I could. But when I could no longer sit in the saddle I had periodically to dismount and lie in the shade of a tree – while my horse fed close by – until I became a bit better. Then I would remount and ride hard once more until I had to rest again, and so on.

Eventually I became so bad that I must have turned light-headed with the high fever. I evidently dozed off, for when I regained consciousness the sun was descending low over the treetops and my horse was nowhere to be seen, so I imagined that he must have departed for home. The only solution was to walk, as I still had about two miles to travel.

I set off confidently in what I thought was the right direction, but in actual fact I was so dazed with fever that I had temporarily lost my bearings and was, in truth, simply retracing my steps along the way we had come! I failed to discover my mistake until I had walked a good mile down to the Nels River, which I at first thought was the Crocodile, and so had to return.

After going some distance my head felt as if it would split open if I continued to walk or even to stand – though it was not quite so painful when I sat down. Finally I discovered that the only tolerable way of progressing at all, with the minimum

amount of pain involved, was to crawl along on my hands and knees.

Fortunately it was mainly downhill from there on, but when I arrived at a spruit just before the Crocodile I found to my chagrin a lot of water, about a foot deep, at the crossing. I attempted to rise to my feet in order to walk through, but immediately my head felt like splitting again, and so the only thing left was to crawl through – clothes and all. I feel sure I must have presented a most comical sight, and anybody seeing me would have been justified in concluding that I was drunk. However, I negotiated the spruit and thence reached the Crocodile River, where there was a pontoon for transporting wagons and foot passengers.

By the greatest of luck the old Zulu, Jim, who used to work in the garden on the opposite bank of the river, had not yet gone home; and he managed to hear my shouts (feeble as they undoubtedly were) to him to call Mr MacArthur, who was living with me at the time. As the house was quite a mile away from this point in the river, I had to remain there in my wet clothes, with a high fever, until Mac arrived for me with the pontoon. He then loaded me on his horse and so took me home. I went straight to bed, took a couple of hot drinks and some quinine, and felt perfectly all right again next day. I feel sure I owed my rapid recovery to my strong constitution, as taking such liberties with a strong dose of malaria would probably kill many people!

During the time I was working for Mr Hall the Magato Rebellion broke out in the Zoutpansberg and I was commandeered to go.

Under the old Transvaal Republic, when commandeered to go to the front, every burger had to have a horse, saddle and bridle, rifle and one hundred rounds of ammunition, and rations for one week. Should he not possess these he had to either buy them or proceed with the "foot-sloggers", which was not very pleasant. I had just lost my own horse through horse sickness so I departed by train for Belfast in order to bid farewell to my parents and to buy a new horse there.

Having acquired one and being already fitted out with the other requisites, I, together with a friend, rode to Lydenburg, where we caught up with our commando, and from thence on to Pietersburg. We were accompanied by wagons which carried all our equipment. Somewhere between Lydenburg and Pietersburg we arrived at a roadside hotel – I forget now what it was called – but as the owner was quite alone he asked me whether I would take charge of the bar, since he himself was unable to attend to both it and the shop. I do not know why he selected me for the job, but at any rate I agreed to assist him; and the training I had received in the old Black Cat came in useful as I could "sling the drink" (as is the merry saying) all right.

One member of the commando (who shall remain nameless, even though he is dead long since) was, I presently noticed, having too much to drink, so I refused to serve him any more, and after the others had left only he and the owner of the hotel remained. I felt disinclined to leave the intoxicated one behind, for he was elderly and I also feared that he would go on the bust again and stay there. After a great deal of gentle and patient persuasion he agreed to come with me and I managed to assist him on to his pony – which, by the way, was one of the best in the commando, even though it had a crooked foreleg. We set off in pursuit of the others, who by that time already were a good way ahead.

After travelling some distance without a hitch, the old chap suddenly fell off. Unfortunately his foot remained caught in the stirrup, and away went the pony with the rider swinging precariously by the leg. I thought he would certainly be killed as the pony was very spirited and was now thoroughly frightened at the unusual sensation of dragging the man. I realised that it was no use my galloping after the animal to try and catch it as such a step would only further terrify it and make it run faster, so I rode round it and then closed in and caught it by the bridle.

I thought old "Paul" was dead, but there is a saying that babies and drunks fall softly! After pulling his foot out of the stirrup he was able to stand, and he was thoroughly sobered by the fright he had sustained. "Man!" he said, "I thought it was all up with me when the pony was dragging me! I started to pray, and every time I was getting on fine with the prayer my head would strike the ground or a stone, and I'd stop; and then I would begin all over again, with the same result, until I saw you standing beside me!"

I would like to mention, in passing, that the little pony with the crooked front leg was the best horse in the commando; he was absolutely tireless. I saw many knocked-up horses left behind; their riders had pushed them on as far as possible hoping to catch up with the wagons, but wearying of the attempt had abandoned them.

A curious coincidence happened in the case of this particular pony; for one day an elderly man happened to ride past, and noticing it he asked "Paul" where he had obtained it. The reply was that he had bought it at a sale in Barberton. The man then said, "You need never be afraid of riding him! He won't knock up because he has my brand upon him!" This man also stated that the crooked front leg was the result of a break when a foal.

There is nothing of any particular interest I can relate about the campaign. There was a certain amount of skirmishing, but the rebellion was soon quelled and we returned home. A few of the men remained behind as the government was enrolling a police force to keep law and order, so I sold my horse to one of them and then returned by train to Riverside.

After working for Mr Hall for a couple of years, I decided to embark on a big-game shooting trip through the country now included in the Kruger National Park. I was away for some while and on my return I was greeted with the news that the Boer War had broken out.

This was distressing news to me as I had friends on both sides and on this account naturally wished to keep out of the war, so I joined company with Bob Sanderson, who was just on the point of leaving with his cattle for Portuguese East Africa. We only just managed to cross the Lebombo hills (the political boundary) in time, as we subsequently learnt that a party of Boers, on hearing of Sanderson's bid to get his cattle out of the country, had followed us as far as the border, where they had to turn back.

Having selected a suitable spot in the Portuguese territory, Sanderson and I built a camp with cattle kraals, etc.; and for the time being we were well content with life, as there was plenty of game about and we had excellent horses belonging to the Sandersons. Then one fine day a Portuguese African policeman arrived at our camp to inform us that we must report to the Portuguese Commandant at Inkomati, some twenty miles away. On our arrival, in due course, the Commandant received us in the friendly and courteous manner characteristic of these hospitable people but said that, since we were now living in Portuguese territory, it was necessary for us to have a permit for the right to do so. In his own currency the amount required sounded alarming, but in English money it actually amounted to only a few pounds.

The Commandant then invited us to a good lunch with plenty of excellent Portuguese wine, and finally, with obvious pride, escorted us round his estate. Unfortunately he had dined and wined us so well that it is doubtful whether we were in a fit state to take careful notice of all the fine things he wished us to see, but I do remember that, his post being situated on the bank of the Komati and having an abundance of free labour to carry all the water necessary for his cultivation, he seemed to be well and profitably established.

When we had set out for Inkomati that morning the weather looked so settled that we neglected to bring mackintoshes with us. We were to regret this on our return journey as we were caught in one of those sudden, violent thunderstorms that, in tropical Africa, have a habit of descending upon one at any

moment during the rainy season. Such a storm comes up with astonishing suddenness, almost at a moment's notice, and within a few minutes everything not under some form of cover is completely drenched, while the violent peals of reverberating thunder, accompanied by vicious, almost continuous lightning, render the experience of being caught out in one of these affairs even more unpleasant – especially if one is on horseback.

In this instance we very soon became thoroughly soaked and were feeling wretched enough when, fortunately, we came upon a Banyan transport rider[3] who was sitting under his tarpaulin-covered wagon, with the water pouring past all over the flooded ground around him. Unpleasant though even his plight appeared to be, it was still one degree better than ours, so we gratefully accepted his permission to join him in his refuge beneath the wagon. Having unsaddled our dripping horses we tied them to the wagon wheel. The rain continued all night, and most "demmed wet; moist and unpleasant" it was, sitting there beneath the wagon and shivering in our wet clothes!

---

[3] Indian trader. "Banyan" or "Banian" merchant was a term widely used in India and countries with Indian immigrants.

Fortunately next day broke fine and sunny, and after the kindly Banyan had given us a good, warming cup of coffee, biscuits and some dry cigarettes, we resumed our journey and finally reached our camp.

One day after we had been at our camp for about a month, a native messenger arrived with a letter from Bill Sanderson, telling Bob to return immediately to his farm with his horses and cattle as the Boers were making things unpleasant for him, so he packed up and bade us farewell, and that was the last time I saw Bob Sanderson. I remained behind with two men – Karshagen and Neville Edwards – who were camped not far from us and who had left the Transvaal for the same reason as ourselves.

## Chapter 3

# STEINACKER'S HORSE

It was popularly supposed that the Boer War would last only a few months instead of three years, and at first we did not wish to move too far from the border, so that we could keep in reasonable touch with news of the war and affairs at home. But as time went by, and there seemed no imminent prospect of an end to hostilities, we decided to trek further into Portuguese East Africa to some spot possibly containing a greater abundance and variety of big game, in the special hope of coming across elephant – but in this we were not successful.

During this venture we were joined by George Bunting, also an old Lowvelder, and when we turned up at Inkomati for news of the war we must have appeared a pretty tough-looking band of desperadoes since our clothes, by this time, were pretty ragged: the legs of our trousers being cut off at the knees and turned back to front because the fronts had all worn out from walking through the bush and grass.

At Inkomati I met the brothers P.W. and C. Willis (always affectionately known to their friends as "Pump" and "Clinkers") for the first time, and they have remained great friends of mine ever since. The Willis brothers had just returned from a long elephant hunting trip in the interior, and at Inkomati they had heard, for the first time, about the Boer War. They were now both down with malaria and on the first day we met only one brother, the other being in bed. We later learnt that the former subsequently told his brother that he had just seen "four white men who looked capable of cutting one's throat for half-a-crown", and I think that suggests a pretty vivid picture of our appearances at that time!

It was not long after meeting the Willis brothers that we heard of a volunteer corps being raised at Nomahashe, on the initiative of a certain Colonel Ludwig Steinacker (self-styled Baron). This Corps later became famous (notorious) as Steinacker's Horse, and it has already been recorded for posterity in two fine books by Colonel J. Stevenson-Hamilton: *The Low-Veld, Its Wild Life and Its people* and *South African Eden*.

Colonel Steinacker himself deserves a few words. He is undoubtedly one of the most remarkable figures in Lowveld history, and to the best of my knowledge there is no existing photograph of him, which is a great pity.

He was a pompous little cock-sparrow of a man; standing some five foot three inches in his boots; spare and wiry-looking in figure and of possibly 120 lbs. fighting weight. The most

striking feature of his lean cadaverous face, from which, under bushy brows, gleamed two truculent black eyes, was a vast and remarkable moustache, which, well waxed and turned up at its ends, extended to some nine inches on either side of an aggressive jowl, but failed to conceal a mouth from which the front teeth, all but a few yellow and broken fangs, had vanished.

He took immense pride in his various self-invented uniforms. His feet and legs were usually encased in smart, soft brown leather Wellington boots, the tight-fitting overalls severely drawn down by straps fastening under the insteps. The heels of the boots were decorated with huge silver box spurs, which flashed and clinked as he walked. When in full regalia, his formidable tasselled sword trailing from his hip, wearing his heavily laced cap, corseted and clad in a long wasp-waisted semi-naval frock coat with enormous heavily fringed epaulettes, he reminded one, as he strutted about, spruce and stiffly upright, of a peacock showing off its full plumage. He was no doubt a true pattern of the traditional swashbuckler.

Well, we decided to enrol in Steinacker's Horse, though none of us signed any papers to that effect. We were issued with new uniforms and this in itself was a relief, as we were at last able to appear reasonably respectable once more. The Corps was well rationed and what we most appreciated after a forced meat diet for months, was the tinned fruit and vegetables that were issued. The only unpleasant part, in fact, was the drilling (about which the Major – as he then was – was particular) since, although we four could shoot and ride and find our way about anywhere in the veld, we knew nothing about soldiering or "drill". We could each speak the native language fluently also, but in spite of all these useful accomplishments the gallant Major was not satisfied and he turned us over to his sergeant-major, who tried very hard to transform us into smart regular soldiers – but I fear with little response on our part.

One day Major Steinacker ordered us all out on parade before him, and then, drawing himself up very jauntily, he addressed us, as follows:

"Men! I vill have you understand that this is not vun dam pic-neek: that it is vun military organisation, and I vill have you obey me! If you won't I'll damned well break you!" At this point somebody shouted out, "Good old Stinky!" (this being his affectionate nickname among us) and the Major's long moustaches fairly bristled as he screamed, at the top of his voice, "Step forward, that man! I'll have you court-martialled and shot!" Needless to say nobody stirred so the thoroughly infuriated Major promptly threatened to shoot the lot of us, whereupon some other bold spirit shouted, "You can't do that," and so on. Such is a sample of the prevailing discipline. Eventually he told the S.M. to dismiss the parade and told us we were a lot of "pluddy ruffians": perhaps he was right!

On another occasion Major Steinacker summoned all his non-coms in camp in order to give them a lecture on drunkenness. He had us all lined up below his verandah, looking down upon us from his higher perch, and just as he was about to address us he spotted a long, lanky, untidy-looking sergeant with about one

hundred whydah bird tails sticking up in his hat. Pointing to this unfortunate individual, in front of us all, he shouted, "Take dose tam feders out of your hat! Do you tink you are one pluddy fowl?"

My first job in the Corps was to make a road from the bridge across the Komati to Mateveskom, and although I had never previously had experience of such work I must have made a reasonably good job with a gang of natives under my supervision as I believe the road is still in existence. While at work on this task I managed to arrest a man who was enquiring the way into Portuguese Territory, and who seemed to me to be rather a suspicious-looking character. I therefore took him to the Orderly Room and although I was never told so officially, I believe this man had some important dispatches on him.

I must mention, in passing, that in Steinacker's Horse there were several men of very sterling quality whom I have always considered it a great privilege to have met and learned to know intimately: such men as Farmer Francis; "Gaza" Grey; the Willis brothers; Travers; the Holgate brothers; Dickson; little Banger;

McKenna; J.Y. Robinson; Kennedy; and last, but certainly not least, my old friend Harold Trollope of Addo elephant fame; and several others, too numerous to mention.

I was now sent on to Sabi Bridge (now known as Skukuza, in honour of Colonel Stevenson-Hamilton, first warden of the Kruger National Park, whose native name this is), which was the furthest post along the line in which the regiment operated. There I helped to build a block house – later to become the game warden's dining room for a number of years – and some barbed wire entanglements; and as there was plenty of game about I was sometimes ordered to shoot meat for the camp and the native police. Little did I then realise that my future was to be so closely associated with those surroundings, under conditions a good deal happier for the game. Drafts of new recruits were always being sent down to Sabi Bridge, and during the summer months their sojourn was brief as they nearly all went down with malaria within a fortnight of their arrival and consequently had to be sent back to the hospital at Komatipoort.

Fever was most virulent during the summer; and a typical instance of how the men suffered is recalled to me as I remember riding one day from Sabi Bridge to M'Pisane's[4] where there was a fort, built by us, and quite a strong garrison. When I got to Kilo. 104, which was then the actual railhead, where a couple of old trucks were left standing (one being used as a store room for supplies and the other as living and sleeping quarters for the half-

---

[4] Mpisane

dozen troopers stationed there), I found no signs of life and the place seemed deserted. Having dismounted, I entered the door of the truck and found all six men laid up with fever, and not one of them fit enough to get up and fetch water for his mates and himself. All I could do was to fetch water from the spruit for them, give them each a good drink and a dose of quinine, fix them up as comfortably as I possibly could, and promise to send assistance from M'Pisane – which subsequently arrived there that same evening.

Kilo. 104 was well known as a bad spot for malaria, and it was not to be wondered at as there was a large excavation within about fifty yards of the truck, and after a rain this held standing water for some time. Mosquitoes, of course, found it a real paradise but, as I have said, we knew nothing about the real cause of malaria at that time.

One day the acting O.C., Major Gardyne, sent for me and instructed me to take a patrol and proceed as far as the Olifants River. He selected me as I had some knowledge of the country, having previously hunted there. My instructions were to seek suitable spots for pickets along the Portuguese East African border; the object of such pickets being to intercept any dispatches entering or leaving the adjoining territories. I took with me two white men and thirty natives, and thirty donkeys to carry our provisions, which we loaded on the train as far as Sabi Bridge.

As the Sabi was in flood we had to stay there for several weeks. In the end a carpenter was sent up with some flooring boards,

with which we made a flat-bottomed boat in which we managed to ferry ourselves and our goods across the swollen river. The swimming donkeys we pulled across one by one alongside the boat; one native hanging on by the ear and another by the tail; and having got everything safely across we spent the next few days in fixing up packsaddles and arranging the loads for the donkeys, at which task the Canadian Perry proved useful – having done a lot of that in his time.

Eventually all was in order, and early next morning we caught the donkeys to put on their packs – no easy task as the natives knew nothing about the job, and neither had the donkeys carried packs before. Anyhow, one man was detailed to hold each donkey while we saddled our horses and prepared to start. Then I gave the word to let go.

What pandemonium broke loose! Away went all the donkeys, each taking his own erratic direction through the bush, bucking and kicking wildly and uttering the horrid noises indignant donkeys do, scattering saddles and packs all over the place: the scene became filled with shouting natives, wildly cavorting beasts and the crash of discarded impedimenta. So that was that! And of course the remainder of the day was spent in collecting the donkeys and recovering the baggage – all of which were eventually found.

Next day we started once more, and this time I took the precaution of letting one man lead each donkey, but in spite of this some of them managed to bolt again for a short distance before they were brought back. Some of the more heavily-loaded donkeys attempted a little passive resistance, simply lying down. For a while we were baffled as nothing would induce them to get up, until Perry said, "Wait a bit! I know a thing or two about pack donkeys that lie down." He put a lighted match under their tails and the effect was as rapid as dynamite! After that the men and the donkeys settled down, each having become accustomed to their new jobs.

On our way we passed several native kraals, the inhabitants of which scattered wildly into the bush at our approach for they were unused to the spectacle of white men, and they must have found our long array of pack donkeys, and men with rifles on horseback, a rather awe-inspiring sight. We managed, however, to catch one old local who knew the country and was able to guide us across the big flats and to the Olifants River, as, of course, there was no road or path. He gave us the names of all the spruits, great and small, but there was one spruit south of the Olifants of which he did not know the name, and so I asked him his own name. It turned out to be Ingotso, so I said that this would be Ingotso Spruit[5], and it retains that name to this day.

When we finally reached the Olifants, we found it roaring past in high flood. After camping on its bank for a week we decided

---

[5] Now the Ngotso

it was best to turn back, intending to search out suitable spots for placing pickets on our way, and the first place we selected was on the Ngwanetsi[6] where we remained for about a week. Here I was unfortunate enough to go down with a really bad dose of malaria, which developed into blackwater. As is well known, this is a particularly deadly form of malaria and Perry was anxious that I should return to Sabi Bridge immediately, but I did not at first fancy the idea of leaving them all, so remained on for a few days hoping that the attack would pass off. On the contrary, it steadily became worse, and Perry bundled me into a *machila* (a sort of hammock slung between poles) he had made and I had to be carried by natives some forty miles back to Sabi Bridge. Atchwell accompanied me, Perry remaining behind in charge of the camp. I may add that blackwater is a very weakening and painful illness, and several times on the way I thought I was for it, but oddly enough by the time I reached Sabi Bridge I was apparently over the worst. Incidentally there were nine cases of blackwater among Steinacker's during that season and I was the only case to recover.

From Sabi Bridge I was sent to hospital at Komatipoort, but as I was unable to recover my strength it was suggested that I go to

---

[6] Nwanedzi

Delagoa Bay where there was a hospital ship, the *Oceanic*, lying in the bay, where the sea air would benefit me. Here I very nearly suffered the unpleasant experience of being killed by kindness, as, after a few days during which I became quite convalescent, I suddenly contracted a relapse of ordinary malaria – probably on account of the moist sea atmosphere. I asked the orderly  for some quinine and phenacetin (aspirin was not known at that time), but instead of bringing this he called one of the nurses who took my temperature and put me to bed, presently bringing the doctor. The latter was rather a youthful specimen and I don't think he had ever seen a real case of "shakes" before; at any rate his face registered a certain amount of concern, as by this time I was almost shaking the ship.

He said that the latest device for reducing temperatures was an ice bath, but as there was no ice bath available he told the nurses to cover me with a towel and to rub me well down with ice. After about ten minutes of this they found, to their consternation, that my temperature had mounted considerably so the little doctor was again summoned, and he ordered them to repeat the treatment. I protested that if he would only give me phenacetin and a hot drink I'd be all right, but he evidently reckoned that he knew more about it than I did, and since he had stars on his shoulders, and I only sergeant's stripes, I had to submit. After the third go, however, I began to get distinctly annoyed and started to swear at the nurses; but they merely smiled and said: "You cannot frighten us: we are old Tommy nurses!"

When the little doctor saw that his treatment was ineffective he at last consented to my demand for phenacetin and hot whisky; and being now completely worn out with all their nonsense I at once dropped off to sleep, perspired profusely, and awakened almost fit again next morning. The following day I was up and about again as I refused to remain in bed any longer.

When I returned subsequently to Komatipoort I told our own doctor (who had considerable experience of malaria) the treatment to which I had been subjected on board ship, and his opinion was that I was indeed lucky to have escaped with my life!

After spending a few days at Komati I returned to Sabi Bridge, and from there rode up to the Ngwanetsi where I had left Perry. I found him quite fit and he seemed pleased to see me again, telling me that he had seen several cases of blackwater fever while on the construction of the Delagoa Bay railway line and every one had died; he had never expected to see me again. And so I once more settled down to the job of erecting pickets along the border. It was quite an enjoyable existence, travelling from one picket to another and down to Komatipoort occasionally.

One day I had just ridden in to the latter town when I saw a lot of recruits being drilled on the parade square. The officer in charge asked the sergeant who I was, and sent him to tell me that I was for that parade. Well! Of course I had to obey orders, and one of these consisted of crawling about on one's hands and knees, doing what is called "stalking imaginary Boers". The square was pretty dusty and in addition to this it was furnished with a well-distributed top dressing of manure, deposited at various times from the constant traffic of ox wagons and mules and horses. To add to my discomfiture two officer pals of mine – "Gaza" Gray and Neville Edwards – happened to be just riding past. Of course they saw me engaged in these undignified antics and they enjoyed the spectacle so thoroughly that they reined in their horses and sat roaring with laughter at me.

This proved to be a bit too much: so when we were finally dismissed I immediately proceeded to the Orderly Room to tell the Adjutant, Major Gardyne, that I wanted my discharge as, although I was in the army, I had signed no papers nor taken any oath. He was smiling as I approached and he evidently had also had a good laugh at my misfortunes, but he said sympathetically, "It's all right, Wolhuter, this won't happen again; you'll be responsible only to myself in future!" So there was no need for me to ask him for my discharge after all.

## Chapter 4

# WARTIME ADVENTURES

For some reason the native police stationed at the pickets along the border had not received any pay for about two months, so when funds were available I was furnished with the pay – which amounted to about £300 – and instructed to pay them from post to post as I went along. The amount was all in sovereigns, which I carried in the wallets of my saddle.

The first night I slept at a native kraal belonging to an old man called Jakalase, but actually I got very little sleep as he and his wife did nothing but squabble and shout at each other all night, and also my entire bedding consisted of a horse blanket on which

I lay as it was a warm night. I made an early start next day, and on my way I encountered a very fine sable antelope bull, whose quite exceptional horns I coveted greatly for my private collection. I was riding a new horse and I had no idea as to how he would react to shooting. Anyhow, I decided to take the risk as I did want that trophy, so I fired and succeeded in dropping the sable in its tracks. The horse, however, had evidently not been trained for shooting, as it decamped into the bush.

Then began a painful and wearisome pursuit on foot, and several times the horse stood sufficiently still for me to put out my hand to grasp the rein, but always, at the moment of contact, the brute would jerk back and gallop off, and this continued until the sun began to go down and I realised that darkness would soon set in. Once that happened I feared I might lose the horse altogether – with the £300 still contained in the saddle wallet. There seemed to be only one, very grim, solution and that was to shoot the horse. Such a prospect hurt me very much, as he was a good horse, but I could think of no alternative under the circumstances.

I removed the saddle, hung it up in a tree, and walked to the nearest picket with the money bags. On my arrival the corporal in charge expressed astonishment at my being on foot. I explained the absence of my horse by saying that it had died of horse sickness – may I be forgiven for this lie!

After the pickets were all functioning satisfactorily I was recalled to Sabi Bridge

and placed on the Intelligence staff with higher pay. My first commission was to patrol along the foothills of the "Berg" as far as Letaba, which place so far had not been reached by our patrols.

I took with me half a dozen native police, and as I was the only white man, and we would be away two weeks or longer, I took two pack mules to carry our food and blankets. One of these mules was a quiet beast, but the other was rather wild and high-mettled, and each of them was led by a policeman. Suddenly the wild mule took fright at something and bolted into the bush, but the fool had for some reason tied the lead-riem round his wrist, with the inevitable result that he was jerked off his feet and dragged helter-skelter over the ground. Presently his outstretched arm caught round one of the innumerable trees dotting the veld and the resulting fearful jerk nearly wrenched it out of its socket at the shoulder. Fortunately by this time I had galloped round and succeeded in halting the mule, but the man's arm was in a bad state. I could not afford to turn back now, so had to take him along with me, but as a result of bathing the arm twice a day it finally recovered. Natives are very tough!

During this patrol, while investigating along the foot of the Drakensberg in the Leydsdorp district, I came upon a tribe of natives living in those parts who informed me that their chief lived far apart from themselves, away up in the mountain where he stayed completely by himself, and that no white man had ever seen him. I told them that I was the Queen's messenger and that it was absolutely necessary that I had an interview with their chief, and after a great deal of persuasion two of his adult sons agreed to guide me up the mountain to see the old man next morning. They warned me, however, that I would have to walk as the path was far too steep for a horse, and that I could not take my policemen as they would not be permitted to see the chief.

We set off early, and after a very steep and difficult climb, lasting about an hour, we arrived at the place where the old chief lived. There, in front of a single hut, sat a very old native man, and this was the great Chief Sekororo about whom I had heard so much. When his two sons came up to him, they both went down on their knees and touched the ground with their foreheads two or three times – a sign of great respect. He was, of course, a big chief who ruled over quite a few thousand people.

As I was unable to speak Sesotho, though quite fluent in Swazi, I had to converse with Sekororo through the medium of his sons,

interpreting from Swazi. He informed me that he had lived contentedly in that little spot for many years, but the reason why he cut himself adrift from his people he would not tell me. I think he must have been well over a hundred, but his mind was still clear and his sight seemed to be yet good.

I have never seen anyone, black or white, before or since, with such perfect teeth; in fact I asked whether they were his own, a question that astonished him as he had never heard of false teeth! I am sure he did not believe me when I told him that we white people could put new teeth into people's mouths; and I was unable to give him a demonstration as my own teeth at that time were still in good condition. He attributed his good health to the fact that he had never eaten meat, never used tobacco, and had never drunk beer or spirits.

He then asked me all about the war, in which he seemed to be very interested, and I told him all I could. I enquired from his sons how the old man managed about food and they told me that every day one of his family, usually a granddaughter, came up the hill to cook for him, but that when she turned fifteen she was replaced by another younger granddaughter, as he would not allow a woman near him.

Apparently his food consisted only of thin porridge made of mealies or kaffir corn[7], but it certainly appeared to suit him, and he said that he never became sick and had never experienced illness. After about an hour's stay there I left the old man, but before I left him, Chief Sekororo instructed his eldest son to escort me safely back to where I had come from and to provide as many sheep and as much food for myself and my policemen, horse and mules as I cared to accept.

The two sons of the chief accompanied me right through my trip, all the way back to Komatipoort, where I bought two good blankets for the old gentleman and sent them back with his sons. From this trifling account I think it will be realised that Sekororo was a fine man, a true stamp of a natural gentleman in spite of the fact that he was but a simple native, and he was greatly respected by his people. No ordinary native whom I questioned had ever seen the chief, and as a result of his great age and secluded aloof existence he was regarded, in native eyes, as more spirit than human.

After leaving Sekororo's I narrowly missed running into a Boer

---

[7] The term used for sorghum at the time of writing.

patrol which had passed through the previous day, but the natives informed me that it had continued on its route and must by now be well ahead. The following day I found myself among the 'Nkunas – a clan of the Va-Thonga or Shangaans – whose chief was Mhlava, an entirely different type of man to old Sekororo. He was, at that time,  a well-built native in his prime, standing over six feet in height and well dressed in European clothes. He invited me into his house, which was well built in the European style and had three rooms, and I noticed that they contained quite good furniture. Chief Mhlava was a very intelligent man of forceful personality, he could read and write well and was most anxious to hear all about the war. He invited me to an excellently prepared meal of curried chicken and rice, but did not sit down at the table with me.

In conversation with me afterwards, Mhlava said that he had turned Christian now and had only one wife, and finally he courteously offered me anything I required in the way of food for my policemen, but when I replied that the Sotho chief, Sekororo, had provided me with all that was necessary he did not seem too well pleased! I heard later that the two chiefs were not too friendly.

After leaving Mhlava's I contracted a bad dose of fever, probably as a result of a chill caught while climbing the mountain to Sekororo's. I continued to trek, but was unable to shake off the fever, and presently I came to a mission station where I was kindly received. The missionaries insisted that I remain until I became better, but on hearing that there were small commandos of Boers in the district I did not like to stay long and within two or three days (aided considerably by good food, careful nursing and a clean, soft bed in place of the hard ground) I was successful in shaking off the fever and proceeded on my route.

After two days' march I came on a man by the name of Jack Sandy, who was farming in the foothills of the Berg. He furnished me with information about the Boer patrols; told me that they were going about in small bands; that they had visited him a few times and commandeered his horse and whatever else they required; and advised me not to linger in the neighbourhood. Moreover, he stated that he was tired of the war and would like to join the British. I advised him to come with me and join Steinacker's Horse, which he did. I then worked my way back to Komatipoort, reported the results of my trip to the adjutant, and returned to Sabi Bridge.

During one of our patrols we heard that Abel Erasmus, the former Native Commissioner, had a cattle post at the foot of the Berg, in the direction of the Blyde River, in the charge of a man called Dan Harber. This was the famous herd known as "bruin geelbek", which Erasmus had spent years in collecting. They were not of any special breed of their own but all were brown with yellow muzzles.

We rounded up these cattle and drove them to Sabi Bridge, as Skukuza was formerly called. On the second day after capture, and before arrival at our destination, a native came in a hurry to report that a strong force of Boers were following us to take back the cattle. We therefore drove the beasts as hard as we could, while a party of troopers guarded our rear, until we crossed the Sabi at the bridge. Here there was stationed a fairly strong force, and then, feeling safe, Captain Duncan, who had been in charge of the patrol, went to Komatipoort, leaving me in charge of the cattle. I lost no time in making a strong lion-proof fence from wait-a-bit thorn bush. Nevertheless, one night a lion got in and killed two of the oxen. Sleeping in a nearby hut I heard the commotion and, seizing my rifle, rushed over to the cattle kraal; but it was too dark to see anything. I fired a couple of random shots, on which the lion broke through the kraal fence and escaped, not returning again that night.

Next day, I had a platform built up a big umkaiya[8] tree in the middle of the cattle kraal, in which to sit up against the lion's probable return. A certain Sam Bowden, a Cornishman, asked and was allowed to share my vigil. We, therefore, just after sunset on a cold, winter evening, each provided with a couple of blankets, climbed on to our platform. About midnight the cattle got excited, which told me the lion must be about. In fact, after a while we could hear him walking in the dry grass which grew round the outside of the kraal fence. Every now and then, in spite of my repeated injunctions to him to keep quiet, my companion would say, "And where be he now?" He kept on shuffling and fidgeting about, then, as a climax, his rifle, which he must have had at full cock, suddenly went off through the trigger catching on a twig, and the bullet only just missed me. Of course, away went the lion, and I was rather

---

[8] umkhaya, a species of acacia

naturally pretty fed up with Sam for his general behaviour, especially as it was most improbable that the lion would return again that night. So we climbed down and went back to our tents.

Next day I started off to Gomondwane, forty miles distant, where, at the end of an uneventful trek, I handed the cattle over to the officer in command at that post.

At that time we were receiving truckloads of horses, mostly imported from Europe. Unfortunately, since they were not immunised against horse sickness, they usually only lasted for about a fortnight. As so many of them were dying it was impossible to dispose adequately of their carcasses, and the usual procedure was to drag the latter away into the bush where, as they rotted, hyenas and other carnivores would dispose of them.

Unfortunately, however, the foolish mistake was made of dragging the dead horses away *above* our camp instead of *below* it, and meanwhile the carcasses became so many that even the hyenas and other creatures were unable to keep pace with this unusual bounty provided indirectly for them, so that the air became poisoned with the putrid remains. Then, finally, came the heavy rain, and all the rotting carcasses were swept into the Sabi – from which we obtained our drinking water – with the result that we nearly all got dysentery. I myself became so bad that I was packed off to Komatipoort and from there to the hospital at Waterval Onder.

The dysentery obstinately maintained such a determined grip on me that I believe I would have passed on, had it not been that one day I was still sufficiently alive to overhear the medical officer, while passing my bed on his rounds, remark to the nurse, "You needn't bother about him – he will be gone by the morning!" and this spurred me to think to myself, "I'm damned if I'm going," and I believe that from that moment my recovery began.

Later on, when I was convalescent, several of us were sent to Pretoria Hospital. We left Waterval Onder in the afternoon, and having been given nothing to eat that evening, we were pretty hungry when we arrived at Pretoria next morning and were shown our tents. I was sitting on my bed with my head in my hands feeling very unhappy and terribly empty, when someone tapped me on the shoulder and said in a kindly tone, "What is the matter, sergeant?" Without looking up to see who it was, I replied, "I'm damned hungry, as we have had nothing to eat since midday yesterday." He said, "You shouldn't speak like that!" and looking up, I saw he was a padre. I then told him of our plight and that the orderly had said we would get nothing to eat until next day, no rations having been drawn for us. He was a good fellow, that padre, for he went off and soon returned with two tins of Marie biscuits of which we made short work.

After this he saw that our rations were drawn, and from that moment we were all right.

One day, after I had returned to Komatipoort quite fit again, I was loafing around the barracks when I received an order to take charge of a big safe containing jewellery and a lot of money that had been looted at Bremersdorp. I took a couple of men with me and we commandeered a railway trolley, and with the aid of several natives we managed to load the safe on to the trolley, my friend – J.Y. Robinson – handing me the safe key on account of the valuables contained inside.

On our return journey, as we were about halfway across the Komati River bridge, a passenger train arrived and only just managed to pull up within a few yards of us. The indignant officer in charge of the train came rushing up, demanding to be informed what we meant by blocking the line, and he commanded us to chuck the safe into the river. I enquired of him whether this was an order and he replied, "Yes", so I told the two chaps with me to tip the safe into the river.

Seeing that we evidently meant to carry out his hasty order, the officer calmed down somewhat and evidently thought better of it, for he then told us to push the trolley back to the siding, which we did, and the train passed on. Later we made another attempt, and this time we got the safe across the bridge, rolled it to a mule trolley that was waiting there for us, and delivered it to the Orderly Room where I opened it. The valuables were stuffed into canvas nosebags and we handed them over to the Orderly Officer, and I later learnt that there was no list of contents of the safe, so anyone who liked could have helped themselves to the valuables.

In due course, I was placed in charge of a picket at Gomondwane's. There were about twenty of us, and during the hot summer afternoons we were accustomed to go down to a big waterhole in the spruit to bathe. Here we used to fool around and return to camp just before sundown in order to receive our rum ration.

One day we received an order to the effect that we had to proceed to a certain spot where we were to join a patrol that had left Komati for the Olifants. However, the evening before we were due to leave I succumbed to a dose of fever, so I had to stay behind with some policemen and guard the camp. On the second afternoon I went down to the pool to have a swim, as usual, and while I was undressing I noticed two objects apparently floating on the surface of the water. At first I thought that they were two pieces of cow dung as there were native cattle round about, but as I watched, they disappeared and then slowly reappeared again.

I continued to watch the place very carefully, and presently I saw the top of the head of a large crocodile rise above the surface of the water. Grabbing my rifle, which lay beside me, I fired and certainly hit the head – though whether I killed the brute or not I never found out. Needless to say, that was the end of all my bathing in that pool!

This particular pool was quite three or four miles from the Crocodile River and it is more likely than not that the crocodile must have inhabited the pool for some time. Had he just not been hungry, or was he too frightened by the numbers of the boisterous bathing men to have attempted to catch one of us? It is difficult to say, but he might well have behaved differently when only one man was present. Anyhow, when the patrol returned I told them about it and the pool was given a wide berth. Several of the chaps visited the pool from time to time, in the hopes of getting a shot at that croc, but they never saw it again.

After embarking on a number of different patrols we returned to Sabi Bridge, where there was now a temporary bridge across

the river. One day the train came along, packed with natives travelling as far as the point known as Kilometre 104 – the natives all being loaded in trucks. Now, the bridge was a good deal lower than its approaches on either side, and after the engine and some trucks had crossed safely, the remainder of the trucks somehow became uncoupled, with the result that they ran across the bridge – the engine going on.

We watched the panic-stricken natives leaping out of trucks into the river as these wildly shot backwards and forwards until they came to a standstill in the centre of the bridge. The engine presently returned, the trucks were re-coupled, and the train proceeded on its way, but I shall never forget the spectacle of yelling natives leaping from the jolting trucks and descending, like over-ripe falling fruit, with loud splashes into the river below!

On another occasion, however, we averted what might have become a real tragedy. The train came steaming along cheerfully and confidently towards the rough-and-ready bridge shortly after heavy rains had fallen, and the Sabi was heavily swollen and in spate. Fortunately we were able to persuade the officer in charge of the train to halt it at the approach to the bridge while we investigated to see if the bridge was still intact.

I walked with the engine driver and fireman (Boyd and "Clinkers" Willis) to the bridge – to find it completely swept away by the river. Had we not stopped the train it would assuredly have plunged into the turbulent stream, as the incline was very steep and the brakes might not have held. After that episode Sabi Bridge became the railhead.

Sabi Bridge was very hot during the summer months, and the thermometer ranged from 105 degrees to 115 degrees in the shade. One day I put a small dish of hen's eggs on a shelf just above my head in the hut in which I slept, and I had forgotten all about these when some time later I heard "Cheep! cheep!" above my head. At first I was mystified, and then I discovered that two chicks had hatched out in the dish – proof that my hut made an excellent incubator!

I cannot do better than conclude this account of my activities in that celebrated irregular Corps – Steinacker's Horse – by mentioning briefly some of the personalities that were numbered on its strength.

There was one individual known as Scotty; of his correct name I was, and still remain, ignorant. His was a common type in most assemblies of men; the rather aggressively demonstrative "full-blooded he-man", self-styled "second Sandow" and, needless to say, he liked us to believe (it might have been true for all we knew) that he was a professional boxer. Boxing was almost his sole topic of conversation, and he certainly appeared to be well versed about all the outstanding boxers of the time. He rarely neglected to demonstrate his muscle (which I admit looked very fine, hard and strong), so we all had a very great respect for Scotty and we were always very civil to him.

One Christmas Day we decided to have our Christmas dinner at midday, with the only place large enough to contain such an assembly being the stable. This building was suitably cleaned out for the occasion, tables were provided and we gaily sat down to our festive meal, which included beer. Scotty was seated on my right and on my left was a little fellow whose name I cannot remember; he was a Welshman and known to us as Taffy.

Scotty drank his own mug of beer and then deliberately

stretched across me and grabbed that belonging to Taffy. Now, Taffy was a little fellow – only about half Scotty's size – very quiet, with arms not much thicker than pipe stems, but his gorge rose at this abominable theft and, to our admiring astonishment, he yelped, "You b— b—, if you don't hand back my beer I'm going to give you the biggest thrashing you've ever had!" Scotty, completely taken aback at this quite unexpected turn of affairs, gaped at him in open-mouthed wonder – as indeed did we all, to see such a skinny little beggar defying the "champ" himself!

This pause was his undoing, because in the next instant the infuriated and valiant Taffy knocked the mug of beer in Scotty's face and landed several good punches well home before the great man could think of putting up his fists.

In fact, the furious onslaught proved so overpowering that to our delighted amazement the mighty Scotty fled to seek protection under a manger, with Taffy following and shouting, "If you don't come out to take the best thrashing you've ever had, I'll kick every tooth out of your mouth!"

He was preparing to translate his words into the appropriate action when Scotty leapt from under the manger and fled through the doorway. Taffy then calmly returned to his seat and several of the chaps who had not yet drunk their beer offered him theirs!

Next day there was a train from Komatipoort bringing out supplies, and when it returned an hour or so later Scotty left with it. That was the last we ever heard of him.

Another lifelong friend I made while in Steinacker's was Walter Dickson. I first met him at Sabi Bridge and learnt that he had been born and brought up on an Australian cattle ranch, but he had taken very kindly to our South African veld. He was the best horseman I have known. There was one big chestnut horse sent down to Sabi Bridge with a lot of others from Komati, and we found out later that all the rough riders in Steinacker's had "given him best", as he had pitched them all off, one after another. They finally had decided to rid themselves of him by sending him to "the Bridge", where none of us fancied trying to handle the brute.

About a fortnight later, while discussing this horse, Dickson said that it was what they called in Australia an outlaw and was thoroughly spoilt after throwing so many riders, but that if I would hold the horse for him while he mounted he would get on to its back – though he wouldn't guarantee to stay there. The horse was a big, strong-looking devil, but I managed to hold it long enough for Dickson to mount, although it reared up savagely and nearly got me with one of its forefeet.

I then watched a wonderful exhibition of horsemanship which reminded me of stories I had read about bucking broncos. The snorting brute leapt, kicked, plunged,

cavorted, jerked, employed every device in its considerable repertory, and finally bucked itself to a standstill – but it was unable to dislodge Dickson, who then shouted to me to bring him a sjambok, with which he administered a sound thrashing while still on the horse's back. That seemed to break its spirit, at any rate for a while. Having successfully mastered this horse, Dickson obtained permission from the OC to have it as his troop horse and he rode it most days, though it was never really to be trusted and always sought the first opportunity to buck.

Eventually this horse contracted horse sickness but, unlike hundreds of better horses, managed to recover and was finally sold with the rest of the horses after the Corps was disbanded. I often wonder how his new owner fared with him.

I have already previously mentioned Perry, but would like to add a few more words about him. He was a very hard case, but honest, and I liked him, so I chose him as one of the troopers who always accompanied me on my patrols. One day when we were encamped on the Ngwanetsi[9] I told him that our rations were exhausted, and that he would have to proceed with pack donkeys to Sabi Bridge for supplies. He promptly replied, "I won't go! You can send Atchwell!" So I retired to my tent, put on my army tunic with sergeant's stripes, went up to Perry and said, "Trooper Perry, tomorrow you will start for Sabi Bridge with ten pack donkeys to fetch our supplies!" Old Perry glared very hard at me, but he finally went without further argument.

In about a week's time he returned with our supplies, but with

---

[9] The Nwanedzi

no rum ration. In reply to my questions he said, "I'm terribly sorry, but I had to go to Komati by train to get the supplies, including the rum, which was in two one-gallon demijohns. There were some other chaps in the train, so I thought I would just open one and offer them one small drink each. That was the end of the rum!"

He volunteered the information, however, that he knew a Banyan store in Portuguese territory – just across the border – not far from our camp, which kept very good brandy, and offered to go over and get us a case. This he did, and to my surprise came back quite sober. The brandy was excellent, far superior to any rum, which was well doctored with tobacco and a few other things by the time it reached us.

One day Perry told me his past history, which was entertaining enough to be worthy of record. It seems that he was born in Canada, of French parents, and his people were farmers. He did not take kindly to farming, considering the work too hard, so ran away from home to join the American Navy. But he found the work still harder there, so after two years, when his ship reached Cape Town, he deserted and made his way up-country. As he had gained a little knowledge in bricklaying he started to build houses for farmers, who paid him in cattle and sheep at the conclusion of the job, as money was very scarce in those days. Having received his cattle, he would drive these to the nearest pub and remain there until he had drunk to the value of the stock and then he would seek another job. An idyllic existence!

One day he was building a house for a wealthy Dutch widow, but she was always interfering and finding fault. He bore this for some time with dwindling patience until on the day in question, when the wall was scaffold-high, the old lady came along as usual and argued with him about the work. This time, he said, he could stick it no longer, and as she was standing just below where he

was on the scaffold he dropped a brick on her head, which knocked her down. Afraid that he had killed her he ran to his tent, collected his things and cleared out. He afterwards heard that, though badly dented, the old lady had survived!

Perry then slowly made his way to the Transvaal; and during the construction of the Delagoa Bay railway line he obtained several contracts for bridge-building, at which he managed to make a considerable amount of money; but he never attempted to save any of it and spent the money as fast as he made it. And then his temporary good fortune deserted him, for his last contract proved a dead loss and, in his own words, he "put on [his] jacket and vowed [he] would never take it off again", meaning that he had decided never to do any hard work again.

He presently settled down to what in those days was called "blackbird-catching" – recruiting natives for the mines without a licence. On one of his recruiting forays he penetrated Portuguese territory where, being without a licence, he was arrested by the authorities and confined in gaol for a month. However, Perry found it quite a congenial existence as he was well treated and, having money, he could buy all the food and wine he required. After his liberation he returned to the Transvaal, but became mixed up with a native called Long One, whom he shot in the knee with a revolver, and once again he had to seek refuge in Portuguese territory for a while until the incident had been forgotten.

The first time I met Perry was shortly after I had joined Steinacker's Horse. It was reported that there was a "desperado" living on the Ngwanetsi and I was ordered to arrest him, but to be very careful as he would shoot on sight. I took two troopers with me and we slept near his hideout, surrounding his hut at dawn on the next morning. As he came out of his hut I shouted, "Hands up or I'll shoot!" He had no weapon with  him but refused to put up his hands, and merely growled that he was "damned if he cared about our coming as his provisions were quite finished anyway". So I mounted him on a spare horse and we took him down to Komati with us, and he was enrolled as a trooper in Steinacker's Horse – and a very useful one he proved to be.

Dear old Perry! After the conclusion of the war he collected a few pack donkeys and trekked through the country now covered by the Kruger National Park as far as Rhodesia, where he traded in hides such as lion, leopard, jackal and wildcat skins, profitably enough to be able to sell his donkeys and buy a scotch cart and four oxen, in which he brought his skins back to Komatipoort, where he finally disposed of them at a handsome profit.

After he had celebrated adequately with the proceeds, he obtained a piece of ground from the government on the Sabi River, and thither he trekked with his cart and four oxen. He duly settled on this farm, which he called Perry's Farm, and it is traversed today by the main road from White River to Acornhoek. He started a trading store and, what with the store and the farming, he managed all right and he was a neighbour of mine when I came to settle on my farm M'timba; in fact, I saw quite a lot of him and used to visit him regularly to have my hair cut!

One day he said to me, "What will happen to my farm when I peg out?" I replied that, since he had no relatives, the government would take it. "I'm damned if they will," he said, and told me to have a will made out, which he would sign, in which everything would be left to myself. At the time I attached little importance to his remarks, not dreaming that he seriously meant them, but as he later referred to the matter on several occasions I finally had the will drawn up, signed and witnessed. Two years later the poor old chap was buried on his farm, of which I now became the possessor – after I had discharged all his debts, which were considerable.

I kept the farm for a few years and then sold it, and in due course it was sold once more and now that farm, famed for its sulphur springs, is the site of the well-known Sabi River Bungalows.

Among the other Low Country hands who made a living by "blackbird-catching" were Stonewall Jackson, Tom Paulins, Charlie Woodland, Ben Hooper and a few others whose names I cannot now remember.

And so the Boer War at last came to a close and, although Steinacker's Horse was still maintained as a border force, most of us began to look round for peacetime jobs. With this end in view I obtained an interview with Colonel Steinacker, who brusquely demanded my reasons for being so misguided as to wish to leave his Corps.

My reply, that I could get better jobs out of it, was clearly not satisfactory and I was asked, somewhat acidly, whether I wanted more money or whether I would like to become an officer (the latter status in the Corps being considered by its Colonel the highest ambition attainable by any human being, and a certain panacea for all ills), but to this I said, "No, thank you." I knew the officers were living beyond their pay and, although unmarried, I had other responsibilities. Seeing no other way out of it and under pressure, Colonel Steinacker finally agreed to give me officer's pay, without rank, and this suited me for a time.

Then one day the adjutant, Major Gardyne, sent for me. He informed me that the old Sabi Game Reserve, as proclaimed by President Kruger, was going to be revived, and that a certain Major Stevenson-Hamilton, at that time in the Sixth (Inniskilling) Dragoons, had been appointed warden to take charge of it, and was looking round for suitable rangers to assist him. Such a project certainly interested me and a meeting was arranged between Major Stevenson-Hamilton and myself.

## Chapter 5

# SABI GAME RESERVE

When I was introduced to Major Stevenson-Hamilton we had a long conversation during which he explained to me the arrangements and circumstances involving the newly-revived Transvaal Government Game Reserve and as a result of this talk he agreed to allow me three days in which to make up my mind whether or not I could accept his offer.

To be sure, the prospect of the life itself appealed greatly to one of my temperament and interests; and yet there was no certainty – as Major Stevenson-Hamilton had stressed to me – at that time of how long the game reserve would be maintained, let alone whether it would become a permanent institution, and I had my own future to consider. After turning the pros and cons well over in my mind, my natural love of the life won the issue, so when I met Major Stevenson-Hamilton again on the appointed day it was to accept his offer of employment as a game ranger in the Sabi Reserve (as it was then called). That was forty-five years ago, and I have never regretted my decision.

I would like to say at this point, that one could have had no better chief than Colonel J. Stevenson-Hamilton. I look back upon my long, and very interesting, association with him with undimmed pleasure; and no superior officer was more loyal, kindly and considerate to his subordinates. We went through hard and good times together, always in a very fine spirit of comradeship.

To a very great extent the world we lived in was a secluded one of our own, in which we were faced with common problems, triumphs and setbacks; and in such circumstances we had to depend much upon one another. Under these conditions official relationships are tested severely, but I feel sure I will receive the ready acquiescence of all my old game reserve comrades, past and present, when I offer this slight, but deeply felt, tribute to our old chief and friend. May the future years bring him the satisfaction and pleasure he deserves!

Major Stevenson-Hamilton (as he then was) offered me the choice of the portion of the reserve in which I would prefer to operate, and so, since I had spent much of my early life in the neighbourhood of Pretorius Kop, and as it was higher and healthier than the remainder of the Low Country, and free from malaria, I chose this as my station. This area is now known as Number One Section of the Kruger National Park.

Having obtained my discharge from Steinacker's and acquired two new salted horses which could stand the climate, I packed up my possessions and travelled as far as Sabi Bridge. Here I was able to borrow a mule upon which I packed everything I possessed in the world. All the money I had saved was in sovereigns, and these I put in a money belt tied round my waist under my clothes, and, accompanied by two of my old policemen (also discharged from Steinacker's) we set off on our first trek through the reserve.

The first day we did twenty miles and on the following one we reached the place of my old friend, Bill Sanderson. Naturally, the reunion was a happy one and we had lots to talk about since we had last seen one another. Bill kindly invited me to make my headquarters there until I had selected my permanent home.

I was now on the eve of a completely new experience, for henceforth I was to protect game instead of hunting it. My long subsequent experience has taught me that, thrilling though the pleasures of shooting undoubtedly are, infinitely greater and more lasting pleasure and interest can be obtained from the observation and study of wild animals, unafraid and uninterfered with, in their natural haunts; and I have never regretted my metamorphosis from hunter to guardian!

My first tasks, as a ranger in the Sabi Reserve, were to select suitable stations for pickets; engage assistant native rangers; and make short patrols with the object of becoming thoroughly acquainted with my section. At first I found these patrols very disappointing as I saw little game. The Boer commandos had taken heavy tolls during their passage through the country, and during my early patrols round Pretorius Kop, where today so much game is to be seen, I would count myself fortunate if I saw one steenbuck, or maybe a reedbuck, in the course of one day's patrol!

Still I was hopeful as I knew that there had been a lot of game at one time, and I thought that it might return, as it had not been exterminated and the open nature of the country round Pretorius Kop had always proved a favourite spot. I also looked around for a suitable  spot in which to build my permanent camp, and I eventually chose M'timba. Having built my huts there, and so provided a home, I bade farewell to my kindly host, Bill Sanderson, and settled down in the game reserve.

Having now my own permanent headquarters on the spot, I began in real earnest to patrol and learn the whole of my section. This work was always carried out on horseback and with pack donkeys – although most of the time I had to walk and lead my horse, as the donkeys could not travel more than three miles an hour. We usually made an early start, and kept on the march until eleven o'clock, when we would off-saddle, cook our breakfast and rest until midday, and then trek onwards until late in the afternoon or sundown – all depending upon when we found water. Sometimes, of course, we had to sleep without water at all.

As I usually had with me only two or three policemen, and they had been travelling all day, I could not very well ask them to chop down bush to make a "scherm"[10] for protection against lions at night; so we were accustomed to

---

[10] A skerm or shelter

select an open spot in the bush for our camping places, making two or three fires near the horse and donkeys in case lions appeared during the night. We also depended on the dogs to give the alarm should anything come around. I carried a patrol tent with me which was very light and did not take up much room on the pack donkeys, but I only crawled into this if it rained. Otherwise I slept in the open.

One night I awakened to hear the dogs barking rather excitedly. It was a brilliant moonlight night, and as I arose to have a look round I could see almost as clearly as in daylight. There, standing on top of an ant heap, only about thirty yards away, was a large lion, looking in the direction of the camp. I grabbed my rifle and fired at him, but as I could not see my sights too clearly on account of the moonlight I must have missed him because he did not utter the usual grunt a lion does when hit, but anyhow he ran away and did not worry us again. Next morning I had to push on, and was unable to stay over and spoor this lion.

I should mention that during the early years of the reserve part of our duties consisted in thinning out the numbers of lions, leopards, wild dogs, hyenas and other carnivores which had not been shot out like the rest of the game, and were now too plentiful in proportion. Every possible device had to be employed to encourage the increase and return of the antelopes and other game, and this included keeping down, without exterminating, their natural enemies so as to give the buck a better chance.

Another night I was awakened by my horse and donkeys snorting and all glancing in the same direction, and as I jumped up, half-asleep, I saw a crouching lioness seemingly halted in the act of creeping up towards my horse, which was tied to a tree close to where I was sleeping. I grabbed hold of a firebrand and hurled it at her, at the same time yelling at the top of my voice, at which she gave a loud growl and disappeared into the bush.

During my first patrol along the Mbeyamede[11] River my dogs trotted ahead of me into the spruit where there were some big trees growing among dense scrub. I presently heard them barking, and thinking that they had treed a leopard (I had seen some fresh spoor just previous to this), I dismounted and ventured into the bush whence the barks proceeded, and there, to my surprise, I found a large kudu bull lying dead.

My men had followed me, leaving the donkeys standing on the bank, and as we were examining the dead kudu to see what had killed it, there was a scrambling rush close by and a magnificent bull sable dashed past, closely pursued, of course, by the dogs – though the latter soon returned. Turning the kudu over we found one wound in his chest and another behind his shoulder.

Examination of the ground round about proved negative, as it was very hard; but I had a very strong suspicion that it must have been the sable that had killed the kudu, though what should have prompted the fight between them I cannot imagine. The kudu had not been dead long as the carcass was still fresh, in fact, I cut off its head and skinned and preserved it, and later had it mounted by a friend.

---

[11] Mbyamiti River

When I settled at M'timba my nearest source of supply was Nelspruit, some thirty miles away, and on occasions when I had to go there I sometimes used to meet some of the old burgers whom I knew before the Boer War, and who had since returned to their farms near White River. We used to have long, friendly talks about the war, agreeing that now the war was over we must all make the best of it and try to get on with each other in a friendly way.

From time to time I used to have several native women working at my camp in M'timba. It was the usual custom when a cow or donkey died to have the animal skinned, cut up and cooked, to feed my big pack of dogs. On one occasion the women, having seen some meat about, asked the dog boy what kind of meat it was. He, always ready for a joke, told them that a cow had died.

They asked him to give them some of the meat, which he did, and they ate it. After they had quite finished their meal, he went round to the back of the compound, pulled out the head of a donkey, which was that of the animal which had really died, and keeping a good distance away, showed it to them, saying, "This is what you have eaten!" Then he ran for his life, pursued by a crowd of angry, yelling women.

Had they caught him he would have had a very rough time for, although natives are not very particular about what they eat in a general way, horses and donkeys are anathema.

The country between the Sabi and the Olifants rivers had now, thanks to the efforts of Major Stevenson-Hamilton, been added to the Sabi Reserve. Since we were very short of rangers I used to patrol as far as the Olifants, where I made a headquarters camp, staying there during the winter months. This old camp was close by where the causeway across the Olifants River is now.

The game was a good deal more plentiful up that way than it was in my own section as the Boer commandos had not operated much there, though I will admit that Steinacker's Horse did do quite a bit of shooting! During the rainy season I used to return to M'timba. The trip, with pack donkeys, used to take about a week.

The country between the Olifants and Groot Letaba rivers had not yet been included in the reserve, and when I wanted meat for the camp on the Olifants I used to get a permit and cross the Olifants in an old military pontoon which had been left in the river there and shoot what meat I required on the opposite side, as I disliked shooting in the reserve.

As I have said, I did a certain amount of lion shooting, as it was part of our duties to reduce these great cats in order to give the game a chance to breed up. Lions had been hunted a great deal in the past, with the result that they were very wild and cunning and we had to work hard to bag them, and I think we deserved every lion we got.

My first return to M'timba from the Olifants came after a lapse of four months and I found that, in the meantime, the town of White River had sprung up twenty miles away and the Milner Government had settled a lot of young soldier settlers there, and was taking out a water furrow to irrigate the land from the White River. Hotels and stores were also being built.

This laudable and ambitious scheme on the part of the government reaped thistles in place of corn, for I fear that the settlers knew little about farming, though Mr Tom Lawrence, who was in charge of the settlement, spared no pains to teach them. The great thing seemed to be for them all to collect once a week at the hotel for their letters and English mail, and as a result of the glorious celebrations inseparable from such occasions most of them forgot all about returning home to their plots till the following morning; the farming had to get along as best it could.

The government, with truly fatherly generosity and indulgence, provided the erring agriculturalists with ploughs, oxen and some breeding stock from which they could get milk, and also a monthly cheque to "keep them going until they had been put on their feet". The money was certainly spent – but not in the manner originally intended!

Somehow there were no visible signs of progress, and after the sadder but wiser government had stopped the monthly cheque the settlers became extremely annoyed and loudly demanded how they were expected to exist. Some sold their cattle, others just walked off and left everything behind, and that was the end of the Milner Settlement at White River. Later it was sold to the White River Estates, and I bought the house in which Tom Lawrence lived while he was in charge of the settlement.

During the summer months I carried out the usual patrols in my own section and it was gratifying to watch the game there slowly increase, especially the smaller varieties round about M'timba such as reedbuck, duiker and bushbuck. All assegais and rifles had now been taken from the resident natives and they were no longer allowed to keep any dogs, so very little game was being killed by poaching.

And thus winter came round again, and back at the Olifants I settled down to the daily life in the veld and here again to my great pleasure observed a steady increase in the abundance and variety of the game; so altogether, things began to look more satisfactory and hopeful.

One early morning, about this time, as I rode down towards the Olifants I saw what I at first took to be two huge rocks away out in the sandy bed of the river. It struck me as strange that I had not previously noticed these rocks, as I had passed that very spot many times; and then, as I watched, one of the rocks moved distinctly and with a tremendous thrill it dawned on me that of course in reality they were elephants! I obtained a good view of them before they disappeared from view in the bush, and I think that these were the first elephants seen in the game reserve.

During the following year I heard some elephants trumpeting in the thick bush at the junction of the Letaba and the Olifants (not far from the present Gorge camp) and on climbing on to some high ground I could see their great backs and flapping ears

projecting above the low trees. However, I did not care to approach too near them as I then had no knowledge of elephants; in fact, to be truthful, I was rather scared of them.

During one of my patrols along the western boundary of the reserve we were following a native footpath when we suddenly came upon the remains of a native who appeared to have been eaten by some wild animal. I immediately halted the pack donkeys and proceeded to investigate what had actually happened.

A careful examination of all available tracks and traces finally suggested the following incidents: a native woman, with her small child, had evidently been travelling along that path to visit some relatives living up in the Berg. During the heat of the day she must have rested under a tree; and having collected a few marula nuts from those which litter the ground nearby, she began cracking these with a stone in order to obtain the kernels – which are quite pleasant to eat, tasting not unlike almonds. Meanwhile the little child played contentedly close at hand.

One can picture the peaceful little scene, so typical of what can be noticed almost any day in the

country districts of the Transvaal. The tap! tap! of the contented native mother as she cracks her little pile of nuts with the stone, glancing casually towards her semi-naked little child from time to time, and uttering an occasional soft remark as the child draws scrawls in the dusty ground with a small twig. Typical vision of African indolence and content – nothing could appear more peaceable or secure!

Suddenly, from the nearby cover of bush and grass, a huge tawny form rushes on to the sitting figure beneath the tree, seizing it to an accompaniment of terrifying rasping growls. The struggling woman shouts pitifully and the screaming child instinctively runs towards its mother, to be crushed instantly with one dabbing blow of a great paw while its owner sinks its eager teeth into the soft still-twitching flesh within its grasp.

This is what the bush signs revealed; the lion had feasted well off both its victims, so that very little was left of either of them by the time we arrived. I pitched camp near the spot as I was determined to avenge this tragedy; and I certainly disliked the idea of a maneater being around. It proved, however, to be a cunning and elusive brute, and though I pursued it for many days it always managed to avoid offering me the chance of a shot. Finally I had, very reluctantly, to give up the chase as my provisions had run out and I had to proceed to my headquarters camp on the Olifants.

Later on in the season, however, I shot a very old lion not far from that spot, and as no more cases of maneating occurred I have reason to believe that he was the culprit responsible for the death of the woman and her child.

## Chapter 6

# ATTACKED BY LIONS

It was not very long after this incident that I narrowly escaped suffering a similar fate myself.

In August 1903 I was returning from one of my usual patrols on the Olifants. On the second day after leaving camp my objective was a certain waterhole en route, at which I intended spending the night, but when we reached it we found that the pool was dry. It was now about 4 p.m. and the only thing to be done was to push on to the next waterhole, which was about twelve miles distant.

Accompanying me were three policemen driving the donkeys which carried all my possessions, and three dogs; the latter all rough "Boer" dogs, very good on lions. I instructed the men that I would ride ahead along the path to the next waterhole and they were to follow. I then started to go ahead along the trail and one of the dogs – Bull – escorted me; the bitch Fly and a mongrel terrier remaining with the men.

Although it became dusk very soon I continued to ride along the path as I had often travelled that route by night during the Boer War to avoid the heat of the summer sun. I gave no thought to lions as I had never before encountered these animals in those parts. Most of the herbage had been recently burnt off, but here and there a patch of long grass remained. While riding through one of these isolated patches I heard two animals jump up in the grass in front of me.

It was by now too dark to see, but I imagined that the animals in question were a pair of reedbuck, as this had always been a favourite locality for these antelope. I expected them to run across the path and disappear; but instead, and to my surprise, I heard a running rustle in the grass approaching me. I was still riding quietly along when two forms loomed up within three or four yards and these I now recognised as two lions, and their behaviour was such that I had little doubt that their intentions were to attack my horse.

Although, of course, I had my rifle (without which I never moved in the veld), there was no time to shoot, and as I hastily pulled my horse around I dug the spurs into his flanks in a frantic effort to urge him to his best speed to get away in time; but the approaching lion was already too close and before the horse could get into its stride I felt a terrific impact behind me as the lion alighted on the horse's hindquarters.

What happened next, of course, occupied only a few seconds, but I vividly recall the unpleasant sensation of expecting the crunch of the lion's jaws in my person. However, the terrified horse was bucking and plunging so violently that the lion was unable to maintain its hold, but it managed to knock me out of the saddle.

Fortune is apt to act freakishly at all times, and it may seem a strange thing to suggest that it was fortunate for myself that I happened to fall almost on top of the second lion as he was running round in front of my horse, to get hold of it by the head.

Had I fallen otherwise, however, it is probable that the lion would have grasped me by the head and then this book would assuredly never have been written! Actually, the eager brute gripped my right shoulder between its jaws and started to drag me away, and as it did so I could hear the clatter of my horse's hooves over the stony ground as it raced away with the first lion in hot pursuit; itself in turn being chased by my dog Bull.

Meanwhile, the lion continued dragging me towards the neighbouring Metsimetsi Spruit. I was dragged along on my back, being held by the right shoulder, and as the lion was walk-

ing over me his claws would sometimes rip wounds in my arms. I was wearing a pair of spurs with strong leather straps and these acted as brakes, scoring deep furrows in the ground over which we travelled.

When the "brakes" acted too efficiently the lion would give an impatient jerk of his great head, which added excruciating pain to my shoulder, already deeply lacerated by the powerful teeth. I certainly was in a position to disagree emphatically with Dr Livingstone's theory, based on his own personal experience, that the resulting shock from the bite of a large carnivorous animal so numbs the nerves that it deadens all pain. In my own case I was conscious of great physical agony, and in addition to this was the mental agony as to what the lion would presently do with me; whether he would kill me first or proceed to dine off me while I was still alive!

Of course, in those first few moments I was convinced that it was all over with me and that I had reached the end of my earthly career.

But then, as our painful progress still continued, it suddenly struck me that I might still have my sheath knife! I always carried this attached to my belt on the right side. Unfortunately, the knife

did not fit too tightly in its sheath, and on two previous occasions when I had had a spill from my horse while galloping after game during the Boer War it had fallen out. It seemed almost too much to expect that it could still be safely there after the recent rough episodes.

It took me some time to work my left hand round my back as the lion was dragging me over the ground, but eventually I reached the sheath and, to my indescribable joy, the knife was still there! I secured it and wondered where best first to stab the lion. It flashed through my mind that, many years ago, I had read in a magazine or newspaper that if you hit a cat on the nose he must sneeze before doing anything. This particular theory is, of course, incorrect; but at the time I seriously entertained the idea of attempting it, though on second thoughts I dismissed the notion, deciding that in any case he would just sneeze and pick me up again – this time perhaps in a more vital spot!

I decided finally to stick my knife into his heart, and so I began to feel very cautiously for his shoulder. The task was a difficult and complicated one because, gripped as I was, high up in the right shoulder, my head was pressed right up against the lion's mane, which exuded a strong lion smell (incidentally, he was purring very loudly, something after the fashion of a cat – only on a far louder scale – perhaps in pleasant anticipation of the meal he intended to have) and this necessitated my reaching with my left hand holding the knife across his chest so as to gain access to his left shoulder. Any bungling in this manoeuvre would arouse the lion, with instantly fatal results to myself!

However, I managed it successfully and, knowing where his heart was located, I struck him twice in quick succession with two backhanded strokes behind the left shoulder. The lion let out a furious roar and I desperately struck him again: this time upwards into his throat. I think this third thrust severed the jugular vein, as the blood spurted out in a stream all over me. The lion released his hold and slunk off into the darkness. Later I measured the distance and found  that he had dragged me sixty yards. Incidentally, it transpired later that both first thrusts had reached the heart.

The scene, could anyone have witnessed it, must have been eerie in the extreme as, in the darkness, I staggered to my feet, not realising how seriously I had wounded the lion, whose long-drawn moans resounded nearby. I thought first to frighten him off with the human voice and shouted after him all the names I could think of, couched in the most lurid language. Suddenly I remembered the other lion that had chased my horse. It was more likely that it would fail to catch the horse, once the latter was at a full gallop, and then, what was more probable, it would return to its mate and find me there, quite unarmed except for my knife – as of course my rifle had been flung into the long grass when I fell off my horse.

At first I thought of setting the grass alight to keep away the second lion. Getting the matchbox from my pocket I gripped it in my teeth, as of course my right arm was quite useless, not only on account of the wound from the lion's teeth in my shoulder, but also because its claws had torn out some of the tendons about the wrist. I struck a match and put it to the grass, but as there was by now a heavy dew the grass would not burn – fortunately, of course, as it turned out, else my rifle would have been burnt.

My next idea was to climb into a tree and thus to place myself beyond the lion's reach. There were several trees in the vicinity, but they all had long trunks, and with my one arm I was unable to climb them. Presently, however, I located one with a fork near the ground and after a great deal of trouble I managed to climb into it, reaching a bough some twelve feet from the ground in which I sat. I was now commencing to feel very shaky indeed, both as a result of the shock I had sustained and loss of blood. What clothes I had left covering me were saturated with blood, both my own and that of the lion, and the effect of the cold night air on the damp clothing considerably added to my discomfort, while my shoulder was still bleeding badly.

I realised that I might faint from loss of blood and fall off the bough on which I was sitting, so I removed my belt and somehow strapped myself to the tree. My thirst was terrible and I would have offered much for a cup of water. One consoling reflection was that I knew my men would find me as I was not far from the path.

Meanwhile I could still occasionally hear the lion I had stabbed grunting and groaning in the darkness, somewhere close by; and presently, resounding eerily over the night air, I heard the long-drawn guttural death rattle in his throat – and felt a trifle better then as I knew that I had killed him.

My satisfaction was short-lived, however, as very soon afterwards approaching rustles in the grass heralded the arrival of the second lion which, as I had surmised, had failed to catch my horse. I heard it approach the spot where I had got to my feet and from there, following my blood spoor all the time, it advanced to the tree in which I sat. Arriving at the base of the tree, it reared itself up against the trunk and seemed to be about to try to climb it.

I was overcome with horror at this turn of affairs, as it appeared as though I had got away from one lion only to be caught by the other: the tree which harboured me being quite easy to climb (had it not been so I could never have worked my way up to my perch) and not absolutely beyond the powers of a determined, hungry lion! In despair I shouted down at the straining brute, whose upward-turned eyes I could momentarily glimpse reflected in the starlight, and this seemed to cause him to hesitate.

Fortunately, just then my faithful dog Bull appeared on the scene. Never was I more grateful at the arrival of man or beast! He had evidently discovered that I was no longer on the horse and was missing, and had come back to find me. I called to him and encouraged him to go for the lion, which he did in right good heart, barking furiously at it and so distracting its attention that it made a short rush at the plucky dog, who managed to keep his distance.

And so this dreadful night passed on. The lion would leave the tree and I could hear him rustling about in the grass, and then he would return, and the faithful Bull would rush at him barking, and chase him off, and so on. Finally he seemed to lie up somewhere in the neighbouring bush.

Some considerable time later, perhaps an hour, I heard a most welcome sound: the clatter of tin dishes rattling in a hamper on the head of one of my men who was at last approaching along the path. In the stillness of the night one can hear the least sound quite a long way off in the veld. I shouted to him to beware as there was a lion somewhere near. He asked me what he ought to do and I told him to climb into a tree. I heard a rattling crash as he dropped the hamper and then silence for a while.

I then asked him if he was up a tree, and whether it was a big one, to which he replied that it was not a tall tree but that he had no wish to come down and search for a better one as he could already hear the lion rustling in the grass near him! He informed me that the other men were not so far behind, and I then told him all that had happened – a recital of events which, to judge by the tone of his comments, did little to reassure him of the pleasantness of his present situation!

After a time, which seemed ages, we heard the little pack of donkeys approaching along the path and I shouted instructions to the men to halt where they were as there was a lion in the grass quite near, and to fire off a few shots to scare him. This they did, then, as they approached the tree in which I sat, I told them first of all to make a good fire, which did not take long to flare up, as some form of protection in case the lion returned: and then they assisted me down from the tree. It was a painful and laborious business, as I was very stiff and sore from my wounds, and I found the descent very much harder than the ascent.

The first question I asked my men was whether they had any water in the calabash which they always carried with them. They replied that it was empty, and so the only thing for us to do was to set out for the next waterhole, which was about six miles further ahead. Before leaving they searched unsuccessfully for my rifle in the long grass. To arm myself I took one of the men's assegais, and then, with the donkeys, we set forth.

Before leaving the place we took some firebrands from the fire and threw them into the veld in the direction where the lion had disappeared, nonetheless, he followed us for a long way, and we

could hear him now this side of the path, now that; but we had three dogs with us now and they barked repeatedly at him, successfully keeping him off.

At last we came to one of my old pickets of the Steinacker days where the huts were still standing. Here, formerly, there had always been a large pool of water, so I sent two of the men with the canvas nosebag which was the only utensil we took for carrying water. My disappointment can be measured when they returned to report that the pool was dry, for you must remember that not a drop had passed my lips since the previous day.

I said that I must have water, or I would die, and told them to take a candle from among my baggage, place it in a broken bottle and with this rough lantern to go and search for water. They were two good men, and off they set once more. They seemed to be away for hours but when they did finally return they had the nosebag half full of muddy fluid; and this they set on the ground in front of me. It was pretty filthy-looking stuff, still it was water; and I knelt down beside it and drank until I could drink no more – leaving just a little with which they could wash my wounds. They proved to be too awkward and clumsy over the latter job, however, and after a few minutes I could bear it no longer and ordered them to desist. Actually the wounds received no dressing of any kind (I could not see the largest wound, which was on my back) until I reached Komatipoort – four days later.

I then told the men to unroll my blankets so that I could lie down. My arm was so painful that I instructed them to strap it to one of the poles in the roof of the hut, thinking thereby to ease the pain, but it did no good, and afterwards I had it undone again. I need hardly add that there was no sleep for me that night, and next morning I was in a raging fever; and though I had walked six miles on the previous evening, I was unable to walk – or even stand – now.

We remained over in the camp that day and I sent the men back to skin the dead lion. I instructed them to return to the tree in which they had found me, follow my blood spoor until they came to the place where I had stabbed the lion, and then to follow its blood spoor for a short distance when they would find its carcass.

I could observe that they were a bit dubious about the reality of my having actually killed the lion (though they had politely refrained from hinting their scepticism) as it was an unheard-of thing for a man to kill a lion with a knife. All my orders were obeyed and in due course they returned with the skin, skull and some of the meat, and the heart to show me where I had pierced it with the knife. They also brought with them my horse, which had later returned to the scene of the accident. It is strange that the horse should have returned after the terrible fright it had sustained, but I put this down to the companionship between horse and man in the veld.

The bridle was broken, but the saddle was intact: in fact I am using the same saddle today, forty years later! The men brought the horse to the door of my hut where I crawled to see him. He

was badly clawed on the hindquarters and we rubbed a little salt into the wound (I should have done the same to mine at the time) and this certainly seemed to stop septic poisoning setting in as a result of the lion's claws. The horse recovered completely, but, though it was a valuable animal – being salted – and a good shooting horse, he was of no further use to me afterwards as he remained so nervous that the sight of a mere buck in the veld was sufficient to make him attempt to bolt. I was obliged, therefore, to part with him – much to my regret.

My men told me that when they opened up the lion they found the stomach quite empty, which proves that it had not had a meal for some days and accordingly must have been very hungry. It would not have been long before that lion and his mate made a meal of me – in spite of the fact that I was pretty skinny and hard at the time!

The skin of the lion, and the knife with which I had saved my life, are still in my possession. The knife is the ordinary butcher's "sticking" type with a six-inch blade of the Pipe Brand, manufactured by T. Williams of Smithfield, London, who specialised in butcher's knives, etc.; and this reminds me of a rather amusing tale.

Not many years after my adventure with the lion in 1903, I happened to be in London and, since good knives were scarce in South Africa then and I wanted to bring some back with me, I visited Mr Williams's shop in order to acquire some more of the type that had proved to be such a reliable friend. There was a typical "bright young gentleman" behind the counter, and when I asked him to show me some "stick" knives he looked me up and down somewhat disdainfully — evidently rather sceptical as to whether I had it in me to be a butcher! — before passing a knife across the counter for my inspection.

His apparent uncertainty about me was even more evident when I informed him that I wanted a dozen of these, but after a little persuasion he let me have them. I told the salesman that they were very good knives: that, in fact, I had actually once killed a lion with one of them! This evidently confirmed his worst suspicions for, with a distinctly withering expression of the eye, he retorted, "Yes; they are good. They will also kill a sheep, you know."

As I left the shop I could not help wondering whether that bright young lad was not already feverishly searching the columns of the Police Gazette to see whether any mad gangster had been holding up people and murdering them with sticking knives! I may add that, shortly after the affair with the lion, I received from Mr Williams himself (who had been informed about the incident), a most beautiful knife, made in his workshop. This knife, which of course I still proudly treasure, is about six inches long and contains twelve different implements, in fact, as a friend to whom I was once showing it remarked, all it requires to complete it is a small forge and anvil.

I may as well conclude this digression by recounting how I came by the original knife with which I killed the lion. One day when I was in Komatipoort I visited the shop of a friend and on

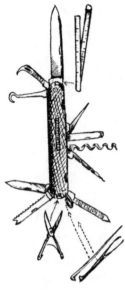

the counter was a big Dutch cheese, beside which lay the knife used for cutting it. I picked up the knife and examined it, as I was always interested in sheath knives. This one, I observed, was the famous Pipe Brand, and far too good a knife to be wasted on cutting cheese. So I removed my own knife from its sheath on my belt, laid it alongside the cheese, and put the Pipe Brand knife in its place. This wicked theft was never noticed as the two knives were almost identical in form and size; and my friend never suspected until I told him years later, suggesting that "fair exchange was no robbery".

But to get back to my story! My men told me that the best treatment for the wounds caused by the lion was to bathe them in the soup formed as a result of boiling its skull, but I remarked that though this treatment might prove effective with natives, it would not be suitable for a white man.

I knew that there were some native kraals not more than four miles away, so sent one man off to commandeer assistance in order that I could be carried by *machila*, in relays of four bearers, to Komatipoort. Having collected the necessary number of natives, I instructed them how to make the *machila* with my blanket, and early in the morning we set out on a five days' march to Komati.

My wounds now became septic, I had fever, and I was in great pain. I could, of course, eat nothing and took only water,

which I consumed in great quantities: two of the natives being occupied solely in carrying it in calabashes, which they replenished whenever we passed any.
By the time we finally reached Komatipoort my arm and shoulder were swollen to enormous size and smelling so badly that I had to lie with my face turned the other way. On my arrival at Komati Dr Greeves attended me, but he had no morphia to deaden the pain, which by now was excruciating. Next day my friend W. Dickson, whom you will remember had been with me in Steinacker's Horse, accompanied me by train to Barberton Hospital, where I received every care and attention.

I remained on my back for many weeks, and at one period the doctor despaired of my life. Once again, however, a sound constitution saw me through, and although I have never since had the full use of my right arm I consider myself exceedingly fortunate in not having lost it altogether. As it is, I can still, with difficulty, lift it high enough to pull the trigger.

After some months I was able to return to M'timba to continue my duties. I once again began to hunt lions and as I had an old

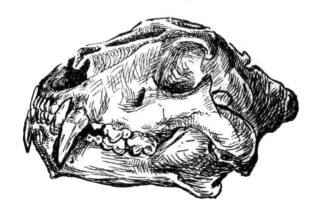

score to wipe out, I think I did so with interest! The chief souvenirs of my grim adventure, the skin of the lion, skull and the knife concerned (the latter has never been used since) are preserved in my house, and they have all been photographed many times.

The faithful and plucky dog Bull, who played so great a part in preventing the other lion from climbing the tree and pulling me down, was eventually killed in combat with a baboon, though the baboon also died as a result of the fight. The old bitch Fly, after presenting me with several good litters of puppies, was finally killed by a leopard. Each of them, in common with many other unrecorded dogs and horses – faithful and staunch companions of the men in the veld – played their part in the achievement of the present-day world-famous Kruger National Park, and all of them deserve their small tribute.

CHAPTER 7
==========

A RANGER'S LIFE
===============

The following winter I made my usual trip to the Olifants River and, in the course of my patrols, found the game still increasing steadily. On one such patrol I had been away from my headquarters camp for some three days when the man whose duty it was to look after my two horses while they were out grazing, must have fallen asleep at his post. At any rate, the two horses had evidently made tracks for headquarters camp.

During the first night they were unfortunate enough to encounter a lion, which, since they were both knee-haltered[12], succeeded in killing one of them. The other horse escaped and made its way back to the Olifants camp, where it was found by my men and brought to me. It must have been thoroughly frightened by its unpleasant experience, as it was very nervous ever afterwards and imagined that it saw lions under every bush!

While my men had set out to spoor the missing horse, I remained behind with one of my native rangers, pitching camp about half a mile from where the other horse had been killed as I was determined to get the lion if possible. Unfortunately,

---

[12] hobbled

though I patiently tracked and followed him day after day, he proved to be a cunning brute that successfully eluded all my efforts to avenge my poor horse. I was very loath to give up the hunt and I persisted while our provisions lasted, until there was nothing left to eat and we were forced to return to our headquarters camp. Indeed, on our way to the latter, "dire necessity" was the means of my sampling an entirely new dish!

We had off-saddled for the midday halt, and although we had nothing to cook I sent one of the men down to a nearby spruit to fetch water. On his way back he found a civet cat fast asleep under a small bush, and having speared it with his assegai he brought it back to camp and began to skin it. I had often heard that the flesh of the civet was good eating, apparently tasting like mutton, and I recollect that in the days when I used to be a hunter, if there was plenty of "game" meat in camp and the men killed a civet they would invariably prefer the flesh of the civet to that of antelope.

I had personally never sampled it hitherto, as the fact of the beast being related to a cat had always prejudiced my inclinations in that direction, however, hunger has a wonderful way of overcoming one's scruples and I told one of the men to cut me a leg off the civet. This I impaled on a stick and grilled over the fire. The leg had a nice lot of fat on it, and when it was sufficiently roasted I tried one mouthful. It proved to be so good that I lost no time in grabbing hold of the other leg before the men had begun on it, and this I also finished. It proved to be not only tasty but good, nourishing fare, and I felt much stronger after the meal.

The civet possesses a small bag – containing a scent gland – under its tail, with the result that when worried by dogs or other animals it can exude a very powerful musky scent as a defence. If this bag is removed when a civet is skinned the flesh remains sweet and untainted. This curious and interesting animal lives principally on berries and birds' eggs.

On another occasion while camped on the Olifants a marauding leopard caused serious trouble round the camp at night, killing one of my dogs and trying to catch some of the others. All my efforts to get him during the day having proved unavailing, I set a trap in one of the hippo runs near the water's edge of the river bank where he used to lie up. This trap I baited with the entrails of a buck. Next morning, accompanied by my hunting boy Sam, I visited the trap and found it sprung. As usual the trap had been attached to a log in order to prevent the trapped animal from dragging it too far. On examining the spot we found that a crocodile had also been there, so we followed the drag, concluding that it had been made by the croc's tail.

After a while Sam and I separated as there now appeared to be two drags, so he followed one and I the other; he thinking that he was on the trail of the log that was attached to the trap, I that

I was on the croc's tail drag. A little further on I saw the end of the log that was attached to the trap; but as everything remained quiet I imagined that the crocodile had been caught insecurely and had escaped, so shouted to Sam, "Here's the trap!"

But when we reached the log there was no sign of a crocodile. I gave the log a tug and as I did so a fearful roar announced the alarming fact that the leopard was, in fact, caught in the trap and was close by, but that he had managed to conceal himself so successfully in the thick scrub that I had been unable to see him. To say that I received a fright would be to express it mildly, and I lost no time in clambering out of the scrub on to a sand bank, where Sam was equally quick in joining me. After our nerves had settled a bit, we crawled back and shot the leopard, which proved to be a very big male with a magnificent skin. His teeth, however, were very worn down, and perhaps that was why he had started to catch dogs.

One evening, shortly after sundown, while camping near a big pool of water on the Ngwanetsi, I was just sitting down to supper when I heard a deep grunt down at the pool. I asked my

natives, who were as usual congregated round the fire, whether they had heard the noise, but they were all too busy chattering among themselves (as only natives can do, when contentedly huddled round the cooking pot after a long day) to have heard . anything. In reply to my suggestion that the author of the grunt I had heard might be a hippopotamus they declared that there were no hippos in that pool.

For a while there was silence again beyond the camp – only broken by the renewed spasmodic talking and laughing of my men, and the merry crackle of the burning logs – and then all of a sudden, and so close that this time we all got an unpleasant start, came a loud, cavernous rumbling and evidently indignant series of grunts: "Heeumph! Haw! Haw! Hee-haw!" now sounding right at the entrance to our "scherm". This latter was constructed of "wag-'n-bietjie" (wait a bit) thorns, and in its enclosed space was my little patrol tent and the two horses and the donkeys tied to a tree.

There could be no doubt now but that our nocturnal visitor was indeed a hippo, that he was evidently leading a solitary life in the pool and might be a cantankerous old codger, and that he had definitely advanced to our camp from his watery domain, obviously attracted by the fire, at the sight of which he was expressing his dislike! The situation was disturbing, to say the least, as I knew that if this ponderous, bulky intruder forced his way into the "scherm" there would be a terrible upset, as the only way out of the thorn enclosure was by the narrow entrance – at present apparently blocked by our uninvited and obviously temperamental guest.

I adopted the only possible course and hastily fired a shot over him. I was relieved, temporarily at any rate, to hear a series of clumsy crashes indicating that he was taking himself off, but my satisfaction was short-lived for presently he returned again, this

time showing unmistakable signs of truculence by pawing the ground like an enraged bull, and I could hear the earth being scattered over the dead leaves. This nasty, threatening display of animal sabre-rattling was accompanied by the usual bellowing grunts and it was very clear that, quite ignorant as he was that we were in reality there to guard his interests, the unsociable old rascal regarded us as trespassers on his private territory!

I again fired a couple of shots over him and once more it had the desired effect of sending him crashing off into the darkness, but this time I decided that if he returned again I would have to shoot him. I walked out of the "scherm" and posted myself behind a convenient big knoppiesdoorn tree. However, the hippo must have sensed what was on my mind for he never returned again and all remained quiet for the rest of the night – though the dogs kept up a great deal of barking.

Later I learnt that, about two years previously, there had been a native kraal close to where I had camped. The same old hippo bull had become increasingly aggressive and bad-tempered, finally charging right into the kraal at night when the fires were lit, so that eventually the natives had to leave and seek a more peaceful dwelling site.

On the last morning before we reached the Olifants camp we caught some poachers with their dogs. There was one decent-looking dog, which I kept, but the others, being the usual mangy, miserable, half-starved type of native mongrels, I destroyed. We reached the Olifants during the late afternoon and I told the men to tie up the dog that I had kept to a tree close to the door of my hut. During the night I was awakened by a howl, and on running out to see what had happened found that my new dog had vanished! All my other dogs were barking furiously, returning to the hut and then rushing out again. Investigation of the spoor next morning revealed that a leopard had crept up under the cover of darkness and taken the dog, chain and all.

While we were deliberating over this, a native arrived from a neighbouring kraal and announced that a leopard had been causing them a lot of trouble lately; and that as it had killed all their dogs and cats and fowls they feared that it would soon begin to catch children. He thought that it was very likely that this was the same beast that had taken my dog, so we started to spoor it. We followed the trail where it had dragged the dog for about one hundred yards towards the spruit and here my dogs succeeded in disturbing it, chasing it up a tree where I shot it. It proved to be

a very old leopard, the teeth much worn and broken, which was no doubt the reason for its taking to a cat and dog diet.

One day, while riding from M'timba to Sabi Bridge on official business, I found no water along the route as it was during a long dry spell, and the first water I came to was the Sabi River; quite close to Sabi Bridge but a little way off the path. I rode my horse down to the river and remained seated on him as he drank his fill, and being very thirsty he took a long time about it. He stepped back some paces after he had finished and I dismounted, getting down on my hands and knees to assuage my own thirst.

Just as I was in the act of lowering my mouth to the water, some guardian instinct prompted me to glance into the cool, inviting current, when to my inexpressible horror I found myself looking straight into the sinister, glassy eyes of a large crocodile, which no doubt had been slowly approaching as my horse was drinking. Those few paces backwards the horse had taken after his drink had in all probability just been in time!

A distinctly cold shiver ran down my spine, even though it was a very hot day! Grabbing my rifle, which I had laid down on the sand beside me, I fired at the croc's head, which was only a few inches below the surface. There was a terrific commotion in the water as a result of my shot, and as the croc sped through the shallows I fired at him again; presently all was quiet as he vanished in deeper water. I then mounted my horse and rode on to

Sabi Bridge — the warden's headquarters — where Major Frazer was in temporary charge, Major Stevenson-Hamilton being away.

Later in the afternoon, when my two policemen who had been following behind with the donkeys carrying my equipment had arrived, we returned to look for the crocodile. After wading about for a long time in the river, which was shallow at this point with a strong current in the centre, we failed to find him — though I knew that I had put two bullets into him. But presently one of the men, climbing out on the opposite bank, disturbed him lying in the reeds when, with a resounding splash, he slid into the water and disappeared.

Another long search followed, the men probing every conceivable place with their assegais, which resulted in the croc again being disturbed among the reeds and again making for the river. This occurred three times; and the third time he ran across some very shallow water and over a sand spit, where I quickly put two more bullets into him. He now lay up in a backwater with his head above the water, and we cornered him so that he could not get away. We threw lumps of driftwood at him, and at these he snapped with such loud clashes of his steel trap-like jaws that even Major Frazer, who had remained at the blockhouse with a bad dose of fever, heard them, and then I finished him off.

When we had dragged him out of the water I found that my first bullet had blown a hole through his palate; this being the reason he could no longer stay under the water, which entered the bullet hole and thereby his throat. He was a big crocodile: fourteen feet in length with a tremendous girth. Had the water been discoloured I would have failed to see him, and he then would have made short work of me.

During those early days of the present Kruger National Park a ranger's life was extremely rough and hard, and there were frequently long spells during which he never saw a fellow European. Conditions in which we lived were primitive, lacking all but the simplest comforts.

During the summer months we had to contend with fever, often being laid up for weeks at a stretch, perhaps in some lonely bush-picket with no assistance but what one could receive from our servants as a result of our own orders. The only available society was our native companions and faithful dogs.

To the average person today it must appear strange that any normal young man could have put up with the life for long, let alone regard it ever more enthusiastically as his profession! But, although the life had all the above and many more disadvantages, and although in the course of it we took many risks, we were young, strong and hard. In the course of our duties it became more and more interesting and we obtained a great deal of pleasure learning the habits of the different kinds of game, in whose welfare and increase we soon began to foster a quite fatherly pride and care.

Anybody imbued with a love for and appreciation of Nature – to which is added a flair for adventure and the open-air life – would have found the life fascinating and the price levied by the

exacting nature of the conditions worthwhile. In addition to this, the secluded and virgin nature of the country, with its extremely few white residents, made of it a little world in itself where there was always much to explore and the possibility of new things to discover.

As I have previously remarked, prospects, so far as the game was concerned, did not appear encouraging when I first established myself at M'timba. One day, for example, when riding across the open country near Pretorius Kop, I became quite excited when I saw four blue wildebeests, as I had never seen any there before. That must have been about 1902–3. Later on a few more came up from further down in the bush; then a few zebra, then some kudu. The latter were very rare for some years (they were one of the species that suffered badly as a result of the rinderpest epidemic in 1897) and now they have waxed so plentiful that, after blue wildebeest, they are the most abundant species in the Pretorius Kop area.

Where now there are large troops of waterbuck we used to see only a few in the spruits. It was actually several years before I saw any giraffe in my section, and now they also are quite plentiful there. Sable and roan antelopes began to increase well, and of course impala, as these were always the most plentiful of all the game, though they were not then attracted to the open country

round Pretorius Kop, the dense thorny bush adjoining the Sabi always forming their main stronghold. At Pretorius Kop I saw no impala for about thirty-five years; even the oldest natives who lived near the Kop stated that there were never any impala there within their memory, while now these beautiful and graceful antelopes are quite numerous in this area.

When I first became acquainted with Pretorius Kop the surrounding veld was quite open in nature, not unlike the Highveld, only dotted about with a few umkuhlu (Cape mahogany) trees, wild figs, marulas, etc., with no smaller trees and shrubs. Nowadays it can almost be described as bush country, the result of "bush encroachment". This change in the nature of the local conditions can, for the most part, be attributed to the rapid spread in later years of a small, stunted thorny tree of the acacia tribe colloquially termed sickle bush. It is a pretty little tree, usually somewhat flat-topped in appearance with clusters of pendu-

lous, feathery acacia foliage, its flowers being especially attractive, hanging in twos and threes resembling pale pink swan's down powder puffs terminating in yellow spikes, so that the effect is two-coloured. They hang like little Chinese lanterns from the branches during early summer. Later it bears a crinkly pod, much loved by kudus as an item of fare.

The sickle bush is very hardy and resistant to grass fires, an important feature in its rapid increase; while the alacrity with which the kudu and other game feed upon the fallen pods – scattering its undigested seeds with their droppings – considerably aids its advance upon the countryside. I am afraid that this tough little bush will become a serious menace before long. I am of opinion that another factor in the gradually denser nature of the country is due to the absence, through control nowadays, of the great grass fires which used to sweep the bush in former years, taking terrible toll of smaller trees and scrub.

Another great charm about the life in those early days was our carefree and simple manner of trekking about. Sometimes with wagon and oxen, and sometimes with pack donkeys, we would disappear into the veld for three weeks or a month at a time. No life could have been freer; more completely untrammelled by "civilised" restrictions; and the very nature of our duties offered each secluded corner and nook of our areas (which each covered several hundreds of square miles of wild bush) and the opportunity to take note of every interesting thing we saw, control of our time and movements being governed mainly by considerations of necessary supplies.

Before I was married I used pack donkeys as my medium of transport, two or three of the latter carrying all my requirements for a month or more. After I had attained the happy matrimonial estate, and my wife used to accompany me, a wagon and fourteen oxen would carry all our requisites for a few weeks.

With pack donkeys one could go almost anywhere one liked through the thick bush, though on occasions when we had to traverse a particularly dense patch the packs would sometimes get brushed off the backs of the donkeys. This I overcame by taking paraffin boxes and covering them with rawhide. When dry these became almost as hard as steel and no matter how violently the donkey bumped up against trees, the baggage remained undamaged.

With the wagon, of course, we had to have a few men clearing the way ahead all the time.

The only road that had ever been made through that country then was the old Delagoa Bay road that is known now as the "Jock of the Bushveld" road, as it was so frequently described in Sir Percy Fitzpatrick's celebrated book of that title. This road was, in the old game reserve days, very overgrown and much washed out, but still visible in places. A great many repairs had to be done to the spruits crossing it before we could take the wagon through, occasioning many a lengthy wait on the journey. Many times the wagon had to be off-loaded at a steep place and the load carried up the bank.

This road skirted (as it still does, in its modern form) that curious, very conspicuous flat-topped formation of basaltic rocks known as Ship Mountain. Many years ago, when the Basothos inhabited these parts, the Swazi impis frequently raided them, but as the former always maintained a lookout posted on top of the mountain, he gave the alarm whenever he saw the impi coming. The Basothos then collected all their women, children and possessions and took them to the top of the hill, where there existed a natural entrance which they would block with boulders. As the slopes of this curious hill are very steep and full of loose boulders, the defenders would roll these down on the attacking impi, thus driving it away. After the impis had returned to Swaziland, the Basothos would descend from their stronghold and return to the flat country.

Wild dogs (the African hunting dog) were a great deal more plentiful then than they are now. They used to congregate in packs of twenty to forty and, as we regarded them as vermin to be reduced without mercy, they afforded us good sport. One day when out with my dogs I ran into a pack of about twenty and, dismounting, I shot three. The dogs pursued the remainder, which presently turned on them and chased them back to where I was standing. I continued to fire at them until I had emptied my magazine – hitting one every time, since by now they were very close. I then took a spare packet of cartridges from my saddle wallet (I always carried spares there), refilled the magazine and shot a couple more, and not many of the pack escaped.

It was quite a common experience for a pack of wild dogs to chase a reedbuck or a bushbuck right into my camp at M'timba. It was really extraordinary how the desperately hunted buck always seemed to sense that I would protect it! I can account for no other reason why they should so often have sought refuge at my camp. On such occasions I would seize the rifle (which was always standing ready for emergencies), and usually managed to blot out a few of them before the rest of the pack vanished into the bush.

In later years the wild dogs contracted some disease – apparently a form of distemper – that killed them off in their hundreds, so that even to this day they remain comparatively scarce throughout the Kruger National Park and are very seldom seen.

One of my pickets was at a place called Doispane's. One day, while encamped there, I was out walking in the veld (this time without a rifle) when a kudu cow came tearing along with three wild dogs in close pursuit. When she had almost come up to me one of the wild dogs ranged alongside of her and leapt up at her flanks, tearing out a mouthful of flesh. I charged at them, shouting as loudly as I could, at which they reluctantly left the kudu and turned back, whereupon I hastily ran back to my camp to collect my rifle. However, on my return they had gone and I never saw them again.

While out on patrol at Numbi I found a breeding hole of wild dogs and returned to camp to collect a pick and shovel and some men. We dug out the pups, which numbered six – though I do not think we got them all as there were so many passages and ramifications in this hole that we could not follow them all. I took the pups home with me, thinking that if they were fed on porridge and milk, like my own pack of dogs, they would lose that terrible, sickening smell so characteristic of these animals. They would feed quite contentedly with my dogs at their feeding trough, which was an old iron railway sleeper plugged up at each end. The scent of meat, however, would drive them almost mad with excitement and eventually I sent them to the Pretoria Zoo, as I had had quite enough of them – and their aroma.

When the pups are old enough to eat meat, their mothers join the pack out hunting. When a buck has been killed the brood bitches eat as much as they can, and then they return to their breeding hole where they disgorge meat for the pups. They continue to feed the pups in this way until the latter are old enough to run with the pack.

CHAPTER 8

# MAN'S BEST FRIEND

Formerly, natives who had already been residing in the area contained by the Sabi Game Reserve were permitted to continue living there provided they surrendered all traps, weapons, etc., and behaved themselves generally as regards the game. Under the circumstances they had to count on our protection as regards their crops and cattle. The crops of those living in my area suffered their worst damage from the depredations of the bush pig.

These wild pigs, which are quite different in habits and appearance from the more well-known warthog, are rarely seen by day. They usually move about in sounders of two to ten, including young ones, and the weight of a large boar might average 170 lbs. – its height at the shoulder reaching about 31 inches.

Unlike the warthog, whose greyish hide is nearly naked except for a long, wiry mane of bristles along the top of the neck and back, the bush pig is clothed all over with a coat of thick, bristly hairs, reddish-grey along the sides and dirty whitish along the forehead, crest and back, and its ears bear long, pencilled tufts of hair. The tusks are short, sharp and businesslike, the lower pair as

keen and deadly as knives and often six or seven inches in length. Possessed of great courage and determination, these African bush pigs are serious and dangerous antagonists when wounded or brought to bay, and many a good dog has been fatally gashed by the dreadful teeth.

Bush pigs are nocturnal by nature, lying up in the densest cover and brake by day and tunnelling through the longest and rankest grass undergrowth. From such inaccessible places they are exceedingly difficult to drive without the aid of numerous beaters and dogs, and their cunning and intelligence in dodging back into cover again has to be experienced to be sufficiently appreciated.

Compared with warthog, bush pig are noisy creatures, grunting a good deal among themselves when feeding or moving about, and when alarmed they rush off, carrying their tails low – not upraised in the comical manner of the warthog. During the night, and sometimes in dull, rainy weather, they visit cultivated lands, creating the most fearful damage since they are most wasteful feeders, trampling and uprooting even more than they eat.

In contrast to the plain-coloured young of warthog, the newly born young of bush pigs display brown and pale yellowish longitudinal stripes.

The adult bush pig, though not quite so bizarre in appearance as the warthog, possesses a pair of conspicuous fleshy protuberances along the front of the muzzle, which certainly does not improve

its facial beauty. Behind these protuberances will be noticed, if you examine them carefully, little hollows, or pockets, and in connection with these I have noticed a curious thing – never, to my knowledge, so far recorded.

Whenever I have shot adult bush pigs during the summer months, I have invariably found these orifices to be plugged completely with the chewed or fragmentary remains of the bulbous root of a plant which in appearance rather resembles a small edition of that known as elandsboontjie, and called by the local natives *nkatzavane*. Among the seemingly chewed fragments is invariably present a small thin maggot, evidently living on them. Obviously the pig eats the root itself, but what the link is between the animal, the chewed fragments lodged in the holes of the face excrescences, and the maggot which lives and thrives there on a vegetarian diet, I cannot pretend to explain; but I have found the facts above related so consistent in the numerous bush pigs I have shot and examined during the summer months at various times, that I feel that they are at least worthy of record.

At the time of which I write, these bush pigs were very numerous in my area of the reserve; they continually raided the

native crops at night and, of course, the natives complained greatly about the damage. What one saw when visiting their lands was enough to break an agriculturalist's heart: acres and acres of mealies laid waste; broken and uprooted plants tumbled in every direction with just one bite out of the scattered cobs here and there. The extravagant habit of the invaders is to test out the edibility of each available cob by taking one bite, and when the result is not satisfactory, to cast it aside and sample the next one, until a suitably ripe one is found, when it is completely eaten. In the process, of course, everything growing is trampled or pulled down.

We were accustomed to follow the spoor of the pigs early next morning, the natives bringing their own dogs, which were held in leash so that they could not chase other game. The same procedure applied to my own dogs, which were unleashed only when the pigs were finally located and put up. The spoor had often to be followed slowly, and with difficulty, for many miles, as the pigs travelled long distances in the course of a night – returning to their daily strongholds in inaccessible deep kloofs covered with thick bush, long grass and boulders.

I need hardly stress that it was strenuous and exhausting work spooring them on a hot summer's day and often, after some hours of this sort of thing, we would come up with the pigs where they lay and before we could catch a glimpse of them they

would spring up in a mass and, with a chorus of grunts, crash down the slopes in one mad rush and so get away. In such a determined stampede bush pigs simply plunge through the dense undergrowth, bearing cluttered and tangled vegetation along on their heads and backs, and so increasing the difficulty of catching a glimpse of the rapidly moving beasts themselves!

Sometimes, however, we were more fortunate, as when they broke out of a kloof and ran up the opposite slope. On such occasions I could often get a few running shots at them and might hit one or two.

Very few dogs will tackle an old bush pig boar, for he is a terrible fighter and if he can get his back up against a tree or rock he will stand at bay and kill any dog that comes too near. I have known one old boar to kill six dogs in succession and then get away before I could blunder through the thick bush and grass to get a shot at him. Once bush pigs are put up and the dogs are unleashed, the plucky ones will chase the quarry, while the more cautiously inclined turn about after a few half-hearted rushes.

I once saw an old boar charge a native who had incautiously advanced, assegai in hand, to spear him where, baled up by the dogs, he stood ferociously at bay. The boar, hackles raised and foam flecking its chopping jaws, rushed straight through the dogs and, uttering coughs of rage, knocked the man down and ran over him. Very fortunately for the man the infuriated boar missed him with its tusks, otherwise he would probably have been ripped to pieces. I have seen a boar strike a dog and hurl him several feet up into the air, ripping him badly with its lower, or fighting, tusks at the same time. These tusks are always as sharp as knives, being constantly worn up against their opposite numbers in the upper jaw.

One day while spooring these wild pigs from native lands in which they had caused damage during the previous night, I

noticed one of the dogs, which as usual was being held, straining at the leash as if he wanted to take up the spoor, so I told the man to take the lead with him, but on no account to let him go. This dog held the spoor well over several miles of rough ground until he eventually flushed the pigs, at which he jerked the lead out of the man's hand, pursued, caught and held by the hind leg one big sow until one of my men rushed up and assegaied her.

I was so impressed by this remarkable performance that I decided at once that the dog would be a worthy addition to my own pack. After a good deal of the usual bargaining, its native owner agreed to part with the dog for the sum of one pound plus one of my own black dogs in exchange – this was considered to be a very good bargain among the natives in those days.

This dog, whom I named Staunch, was a very powerfully built animal of no particular breed, red in colour. I never regretted my bargain and for many years I used him when hunting bush pig. When following them he always became very excited and it was all the man who held his leash could do to prevent him from getting away. In fact, on some occasions he often did break away in spite of all efforts to hold him, which always alarmed me as he was too valuable to risk his being killed.

Actually I had only one native sufficiently strong to hold him when really excited – a powerfully built, big policeman rejoicing in the name of Sixpence. In order to prevent the dog pulling the leash out of his hand, Sixpence was accustomed to tie the ends of the leash round his wrist and one day, when we put up a pig in some very dense scrub, Staunch jerked Sixpence off his feet and dragged him for quite some distance before he came to a stop. Sixpence emerged very crestfallen from his ordeal, but in spite of his rough-and-tumble he had stoutly succeeded in preventing the dog from breaking away.

I bred several litters of pups from Staunch, but as usual when breeding from a mongrel one could never anticipate what the progeny would turn out – either in appearance or character. He was really a remarkable "pig" dog and once settled on such a spoor he completely ignored any other, no matter how fresh, that happened to cross the line.

Staunch was also, unfortunately, a great fighter – though never a bully. Among my pack, which sometimes numbered as many as twenty-five individuals, there was not one dog capable of standing up to him and consequently he was very soon accepted by the others as "boss" of the pack. Some time later I was offered a fine bull terrier whose owner was anxious to part with it because it was a vicious fighter and had the reputation of having killed several dogs. In other respects it was a good dog and though I was rather anxious about my Staunch, I finally agreed to risk serious trouble and took it over.

For several days following the bull terrier's arrival among my pack, Staunch and he growled threateningly at each other, with the usual hostile bristling and contemptuous scratching of hind feet, but at first I was relieved to see that they refrained from actual battle. Then one night I was awakened by sounds of gasping and deep breathing outside my window and on rushing out I found that the inevitable clash of wills had come and Staunch and the bull terrier were locked in grimly silent and apparently mortal combat. The latter had hold of Staunch by the shoulder and Staunch in turn had hold of the terrier by the root of his ear, which was always his favourite fighting hold.

I seized the sjambok and tried to separate them, but it was no use; they just maintained a determined grip of each other, the silence broken only by their deep breathing. In desperation I called up my policemen to assist me to try and separate the two dogs – neither of whom I wished to lose. Fortunately both dogs were wearing collars and I caught hold of Staunch by his, inserted a stick through it and twisted it so as to choke him, and told the men to do the same with the terrier, and that was how we eventually separated them.

I kept them both chained up for several days, but as soon as they were released they attacked each other again and regretfully I realised that, since they had to live together, the only thing left was to let them fight it out. In the end, out of pity for the bull terrier, I gave him away to a friend as both his ears were badly chewed and his spirit quite broken. After many years Staunch grew old and lost some of his teeth, and one night some of his own sons tackled him a little distance from the house and killed him. Next morning we found his dead body; the fight had taken place too far from the house to be heard and the poor old fellow was too ancient then to defend himself effectively.

Staunch was never an affectionate dog and he took no notice of grown-ups, though curiously enough he was fond of small children. I remember some of my sisters once visiting M'timba and bringing with them their small children. They asked me whether it was quite safe for the children to play about in the yard with so many rough-looking dogs about, and I replied that the other dogs were quite safe and reliable, but that it would be advisable not to approach Staunch as he was bad-tempered. A few days later my blood was momentarily frozen by the sight of one of the children actually riding upon the redoubtable and awesome Staunch who, strangely enough, seemed to be enjoying his new employment as much as the children themselves! After that, Staunch remained their best friend.

Among my dogs was an Irish terrier, whom I called Pat – one of the pluckiest dogs I have ever owned. He was only three-quarters bred Irish terrier, but he was really an outstanding dog, knew not the meaning of fear and, like the Irish themselves, dearly loved a free fight! Whenever a glorious compound canine flurry took place you might be sure that Pat would be enjoying himself hugely in the thick of it, and often I had to run out with a sjambok and whip about among the combatants to end it.

One day I happened to be some distance from the homestead when such a free fight began and Pat, as usual, was soon in the centre of it – each of the dogs getting hold of as big a piece of him as possible. When I reached the scene the fight was over and Pat apparently dead. I ordered one of my men to take him away, dig a hole, and bury him. But while his grave was still being dug

the pugnacious Pat revived and, after a few preliminary twitches, he very groggily rose to his feet, flew at the nearest dog and had to be pulled off!

I knew that the next time he became involved in one of these fights he would certainly be killed, so I very reluctantly and regretfully sent him to one of my policemen's kraals, about two miles from the homestead, where I knew he would be well looked after. But I fear my well-meaning attempts to turn Pat into a pacifist failed, because from time to time he left the kraal to come and stand right in the gateway of my yard, barking defiantly, until my pack of dogs would rush out and get hold of him, only to be pulled off by the policemen. Of course the inevitable occasion arrived when only my cook was in camp, and that was the end of poor old Pat.

While on this subject of dogs, I must mention a few of the more remarkable characters among the many dogs I have owned, all of whom have assisted me greatly in my duties and played their small but expressive parts in the saga of the Kruger National Park.

The bitch Fly I have already mentioned in the account of my adventure with the lion. She also was a mongrel, somewhat resembling a deerhound in build. I took her from some Boer wagons we had captured during the South African war on one of my patrols along the Olifants. She subsequently accompanied me

on all my other patrols during the war, and she proved herself to be most useful in tracking wounded game.

Fly would never get too far out of sight when following spoor and if, when so occupied, she had gone sufficiently far ahead to lose sight of me she would wait until I caught up with her and would then proceed slowly once more. This intelligent behaviour she had probably been taught by her former owner.

She was, indeed, very intelligent, as the following facts will indicate. On our patrols during the war we naturally disliked and avoided making our movements more conspicuous than necessary as there were plenty of small parties of Boers manoeuvring about the country. Now Miss Fly liked to help herself to anything going in the way of food on all occasions, including the contents of the natives' cooking pots, but when caught in such acts of vandalism she was chased and forced to disgorge her booty. So she presently hit upon a most ingenious plan, and this was to run barking loudly into the veld when righteously pursued on such thieving occasions.

I need hardly indicate the sole form of appeasement adequate to silence this most unpleasantly noisy and attention-drawing manoeuvre upon her part; and after one or two experiences of this sort Fly was able to help herself to whatever she liked: nobody dared to chase her off in case she started barking and so revealed us to the enemy. When I left Steinacker's and embarked on my career in the game reserve I brought Fly with me and she again accompanied me on all my patrols, but she eventually got killed by a leopard on the Ngwanetsi River.

Crocodiles, of course, account for many rangers' dogs in the Kruger National Park.

Another favourite dog of mine was a big cross-bred Great Dane-mastiff called Wolf, which I bought originally from an engine driver at Nelspruit. After he had been in the veld for a

while he became quite good with lions. One day, while patrolling along the Isweni Spruit, Wolf, as it was a very hot day, ran down to a big pool of water. I followed him, being rather afraid that there might be crocodiles in this pool. He reached the water first and jumped in to cool himself.

Before I could get there I heard a howl and knowing what that meant I rushed down to the edge, but all I saw was a ripple on the surface. Hastily I fired two shots into the water below the ripple and presently Wolf's head appeared on the surface and he swam out. To this day I do not know whether I hit that croc or whether the concussion of the bullet in the water made him release the dog. Fortunately he could not have been a very big crocodile, because though there were quite a number of punctures on his hindquarters and hind legs, none of them were very deep. This should have proved a lesson to Wolf, but in the following year, while patrolling the Olifants, the same thing occurred, only this time it must have been a big croc for I never saw Wolf again.

A very remarkable little companion of mine was an Airedale bitch named Biddy. She was a very small specimen of the breed, but excellent at spooring lions; and at this work she saved myself and my native trackers many hours of tedious labour. She would hold to any lion spoor up to twenty-four hours old with ease

(never allowing herself to be distracted by any other spoor), which means a lot in the dry climate of South Africa.

She was always led on a leash by one of my trackers and on such occasions we must have presented an amusing spectacle, as first along the line would come Biddy, followed by the man holding her, then myself, then finally two or more policemen. On one occasion she led us about fifteen miles before we came to the lion. She was never left off the leash until the latter had been shot, as she was much too valuable to me to risk her being hurt or killed. Once satisfied that the lion was dead, I would let Biddy loose and she would tear away ferociously at the carcass until she had tired herself out, then she would rest under a tree while the men removed the skin.

Biddy had one fault at her work and unfortunately this was rather a bad one. When the scent became hot she was unable to keep her mouth shut and would give tongue in excited little whimpering barks, meanwhile straining eagerly at her leash; and I soon learnt that her behaviour thus indicated that the lion – or lions – was now close at hand. Unfortunately her excited whimpering invariably aroused the lions too, and in many cases they would be up and away into the bush before I could attempt a shot. I tried many ways to quieten her, but to no purpose as she could not control her excitement, and usually the only course to pursue in the hopes of getting in a quick shot later was to sit down for an hour or more and allow the scent to get cold, before setting her on the trail again.

In this way Biddy found many lions for us. When the sun got very hot she would leave the spoor and make for the nearest shady tree, and we had to do likewise. I would give her a drink of cool water, poured from my water bottle into my hat, and then bathe her head. As soon as she felt sufficiently refreshed she would start off on the spoor once more.

Biddy proved herself to be a very true and lovable companion, and many happy days in the veld were spent with her, before alas! there appeared in the Lowveld a mysterious canine disease which had worked its way up from the south.

It was something quite new to my experience, being neither distemper nor biliary fever, but it killed hundreds of native dogs at the kraals as it advanced. Eventually this disease reached M'timba and I was finally left with only two out of twenty-eight dogs. My faithful Biddy was among those that died. I nursed her as I had never nursed a dog before, but in vain. In her deliriums she used to wander about the yard, for all the world as if she was again on a lion spoor: sometimes uttering those little whimpery barks she used to give at such times. But she became in such a bad way that I knew she could never recover, and there seemed only one decent way of discharging my debt for long and faithful service and companionship. I sent her to the happy hunting grounds, where I feel sure I shall find her awaiting me.

Another very good lion dog of mine was one called Grip – given to me by my old friend "Pump" Willis. He was what is known in Afrikaans as a *steekbaard*; a large, powerful breed. Grip took to lion hunting from the very start and whenever we found lions he always bayed up one and kept it there until I galloped up and shot it.

One night lions killed several head of cattle on my farm De Rust, which was about four miles from the boundary of the game reserve. My natives came to report so I put Grip in my car and drove to where the cattle had been killed, as I had sent my horse on ahead. Incidentally, Grip always understood that when he was put in the car it meant lion work, which he dearly loved! In due course we followed the spoor of the lions, which led straight back to the Park boundary. Having crossed this they had made straight for Numbi, which is a hill composed of big boulders and covered with very dense bush, and here they had elected to lie up.

It was not long before Grip put them up and he held one at bay for quite half an hour, as it took me a long time to crawl and fight my way through the bush and rough ground, my horse being left outside. Grip continued to bark all the time, indicating to me the correct direction. The lion, which had sought refuge in very thick scrub, repeatedly made short rushes at him, which the dog managed always cleverly to avoid.

It was, in fact, some time before I saw my way clear to place a fatal bullet into the lion, and by this time Grip was so exhausted and desperately thirsty that I thought he would die. However, after I had offered him a drink of water poured into my hat from a calabash carried by one of the men, he revived sufficiently to set off on the trail of the second lion, which he also successfully bayed for me to shoot.

Grip was a really good lion dog, but like most good lion dogs he eventually got killed by a lion in the end. He had, however, one

Top: Midday siesta near the Ngwanetsi.
Above: Impala at mating time, Sabi River.

Top: Klipspringers, Pretorius Kop.
Above: Kudu bulls, Pretorius Kop.

Top: Waterbuck, Gudzane Spruit.
Above: "I began to feel very cautiously for his shoulder."

Top: The leading dog leapt at her flank.
Above: Wildebeest bulls, Manunge.

Top: Cheetah and ostriches, Isweni Flats.
Above: Giraffes.

Top: Scavengers.
Above: Baboons, Chapman's zebra and blue wildebeest, Ngwanetsi River.

TOP: Elephant bulls and roan antelopes, Letaba River.
ABOVE: Sable antelopes, Tshokwane River.

Top: Wild dogs after the hunt.
Above: "Desperately I pulled back the bolt."

very serious fault: he was unable to resist chasing and killing sheep and goats. At this time the portion which is now native reserve was thickly populated with natives and their stock, among which were sheep and goats. On several occasions while out riding with my dogs we would pass flocks of them grazing at a distance, and once he had noticed these Grip would vanish from my view and sneak off in their direction.

I say "sneak" off because he knew he was doing wrong, having already received several thrashings from me for this sort of fun, but he evidently deemed the sport well worth the price. Before I had time to ride up I would hear the distressed bleating all round, and on arriving at the scene would find the usual dismal spectacle of several dead victims. Grip was a very powerful dog, and one bite in the neck was sufficient to kill a sheep.

The results of these escapades were more paying-up from myself to indignant owners, and a severe thrashing for Grip, but of the two it seemed that I was the worst sufferer. On occasions when we came suddenly on to sheep, and I had to ride right through them, Grip would trot along soberly with his tail in the air, never deigning them so much as a glance, though I knew well that he was watching me out of the corner of his eye all the while.

I bred some good pups from Grip, but like their father they have now all gone to the happy hunting ground.

In the days I used to maintain large packs of dogs I must admit that they proved often to be rather a trial as they were always scrapping among themselves, and one rarely got a good night's rest! One dog would fancy he heard or smelt something and start to bark. This, of course, set the whole lot off, and round and round the yard they would

scamper, barking and creating a terrible row until finally it would end up in a free fight, and I was constrained to leap out of bed, hurling unmentionable epithets at the disturbers of my troubled repose, and set about them with sjambok. The first individual within range would let out a yelp and that would – temporarily at least – silence the remainder.

In addition to these I always had several bitches with pups, and my friends often used to send me dogs which they no longer wanted themselves. Some of these gifts turned out all right, others proved useless, but I usually kept them as by that time I had some cattle, had plenty of milk and grew my own mealies, which were ground into mealie meal, so that my dogs did not cost me much to feed.

Later the government built me a house of wood and iron. It was the third time that this particular building had been erected, but it was a home and a palace compared with the simple wattle-and-daub huts I had been living in hitherto. This house was built on piles off the ground, and my dogs of course considered that it had been built for their exclusive benefit for they all crowded in under the piles to sleep the night. Frequently at night the invariable scrapping and fearful noise would begin, and the constant bumping up against the flooring boards added to my discomfiture.

Very soon they introduced fleas to the establishment, and these unspeakable insects increased at an alarming rate and for a long time they beat me. Then suddenly I hit upon a most ingenious

plan. I had a lot of native boys working for me, and I offered them sixpence each if they would strip naked (not an unduly embarrassing position for them in those days), crawl under the house, stay there for a few minutes until they had collected a bodyful of fleas each, and then run into the veld and brush them off; the operation to be repeated ad lib until I considered that they had transported a considerable proportion of the offenders.

They issued from the nether regions of the house literally black with fleas, which they appeared to consider grand fun and highly diverting, and thoroughly enjoyed this new task. This procedure certainly reduced the fleas considerably, though it did not completely eliminate them. I recommend the scheme for what it may be worth to those, in similar circumstances, harassed by fleas!

Finally I got rid of the fleas with locust poison, and then fenced in the house.

In concluding this chapter let me say that dogs are man's most faithful friends. No matter how he may ill-treat them, starve them or beat them, they will always remain faithful to their owner. On several occasions I have picked out two or three decent-looking mongrels from a pack of dogs taken from captured poachers – the rest of course always being destroyed. These dogs are usually literally skin and bone and often full of mange. I would feed them up, cure their mange and get them into good condition, meanwhile petting them and being as friendly as possible.

They appeared to become fond of me but they never really forgot their old masters, and would frequently run back to the kraal from which they originally came, where they had been starved, beaten and neglected. In spite of all that, and the pleasanter life I offered them, they still remained faithful to the old master!

## Chapter 9

# POACHERS

In 1910, sheep farmers from the Highveld – commonly known as "trek-boers" – received permission from the government to winter their sheep in the game reserve. Each individual was allotted so many thousand morgen, for the use of which he paid £5 to the government. This was, of course, a remarkably good bargain for the sheep farmers; elsewhere they would have had to pay about £50 for the rental of a similar amount of grazing.

Most of these lots had been surveyed and beacons erected many years previously, and during the course of my wanderings in the veld I had discovered quite a number of the beacons and so now had an idea where to look for them. On occasions great arguments occurred as to the correct boundaries and on two instances there were stand-up fights between the dissenting parties. To myself fell the sometimes unpleasant task of settling such disputes and pronouncing final judgment.

That such a role was strewn with difficulties for the unwary can be realised when I recall one instance when I found that the beacon in question had "moved" for a distance of about a quarter of a mile. The reason for this curious phenomenon, I
subsequently discovered, was that the party responsible had discovered a nice patch of green "brand" (fresh young grass growing in a previously burnt area), which he decided was highly desirable for his lambing ewes.

Unfortunately, however, Supreme Authority – in the visible form of myself – here had to step in and, in spite of my resulting evident unpopularity (well voiced with accompanying suggestions to the effect that "I didn't know my job," etc.), the gentleman concerned was politely but firmly induced to re-establish that particular piece of artificial scenery in its rightful place once more.

This state of affairs was permitted to continue for some years, but of course it was not a very satisfactory arrangement where a game reserve is concerned and quite a few head of game managed to get shot every year, nor was it at all easy to get a conviction. Moreover, the trek-boers would first of all set about burning off all the grass in their areas to ensure fresh new growth for their grazing.

The concession was, however, not by any means so advantageous to the farmers themselves as the cheap price would indicate. Just at that time there was a severe drought in the Cape Colony: sheep were dying in thousands and they could be bought for practically nothing. One enterprising farmer went to the Cape and bought between three to four thousand sheep. Having acquired the necessary trucks he railed the sheep as far as Nelspruit. Then they were driven by road to the winter grazing in the game reserve. A large number died during the journey by road and when the survivors reached the Sigaas they were of course unaccustomed to the nice green "brand" there and, in addition, were not immune to bluetongue and various other local Lowveld sheep diseases. The result was that in the end the unfortunate farmer lost practically his whole flock.

In the game reserve, too, lions and wild dogs took a heavy annual toll on the sheep, though the graziers were of the opinion that the cheapness of the grazing offset such losses.

Visitors to the Kruger National Park often express surprise at the rarity of tragedies among the comparatively few humans dwelling in this vast solitude of wild animals and primitive conditions. From time to time, however, unwitnessed tragedies do occur, and the following episode, which happened about three years ago, will serve as an example.

One day three small native children, from a kraal in the Park, were sent on an errand to one in the neighbouring native reserve. It appears that, after travelling for about a mile, the youngest child – a little girl of about three years – was told by her companions to turn back, while they would proceed and deliver the message. The latter was, in due course, accomplished, and the two elder children returned home to their kraal – only to find that their little sister had not arrived. As it was by now already dark, nothing further could be done until the following morning.

As early as possible next day all the inhabitants of the kraal turned out to search for the missing child. At length one of the searchers picked up the child's spoor, but it was leading in the wrong direction and it was clear that the child must have lost her way. The spoor was followed carefully throughout the remainder of that day, but unfortunately it traversed hard and dry ground, with the result that it proved hard to distinguish and progress was very slow indeed. Frequently the tracks were quite lost temporarily and about an hour or more would be expended in retracing them.

Finally darkness overshadowed the bush once more and the search party had to return home for the night. First thing next day the search was renewed, but with the same disappointing result, though during this day they found where the child had crossed a small spruit, and there was visible evidence of where she had knelt to drink. Being so young a child, with very small, light feet and of course barefooted, the trail she left was very slight.

At this point the incident was reported to me. I issued instructions to the inhabitants of every kraal in the neighbourhood to turn out and comb the surrounding country, and also ordered all my native rangers to join in the search. If, indeed, still alive, the poor little thing must by now have been in a pretty bad way, having had nothing to eat for two days and having travelled all the time.

A touching picture can be conjured up in the imagination of this small, scantily clad human waif, desperately and ever more weakly trudging hopelessly about throughout this vast, dry and inhospitable bush country – perhaps at night seeking fearful refuge in accommodating antbear holes or rock crevices, listening with lonely terror to the reverberating roaring of lions, the shrill, fierce crying of jackals, or the eerie moaning wails of hyenas.

A situation sufficiently fraught with horror to test the nerves of the most hardened individual, let alone those of a mere three-year-old!

I supervised the search personally on horseback. On the fourth day we again found the spoor in a big sandy spruit called Pabin. Here was some water, and the child had again drunk. By this time

the faint tracks simply led backwards and forwards in an aimless fashion. On the following day we found hyena spoor superimposed over that of the child, but whether the great spotted scavenging brute had actually been following the child it was hard to tell.

Anyhow, shortly after that the spoor became finally lost forever, and though we searched everywhere until nightfall we were compelled in the end to give it up, and the exact nature of the end of the tragedy remains a mystery; yet one more to the many thousands locked away and unrevealed in the loneliness of the African bush. The little mite may have succumbed to starvation and weakness in some secluded hollow, or hyena or lion may have cut short the drawn-out agony – this latter possibility probably proving the quickest and most merciful conclusion of all.

Natives from the native reserve, which joins the Park, sometimes cause a lot of trouble by crossing the Park boundary and killing game, sometimes with their dogs and sometimes with rifles which they somehow manage to acquire but never keep at their own kraals. The rifles, in fact, are usually hidden in hollow trees, in caves or under rocks – with the result that the stocks are usually white ant eaten and the barrels pitted with rust. Nevertheless they seem good enough to fire a cartridge and kill a buck at short distance.

Personally I would not attempt to fire one of these weapons at any price in case they should burst, the insides of the barrels being invariably choked with rust and dirt. I have often asked these poachers, when they have been caught, why they do not use a pull-through and keep the grooves clean, and their usual reply is that "they shoot better that way".

At one time when a band of poachers, disturbed by my native rangers, cleared off into the bush the usual method of halting them was for the native rangers to fire a couple of shots into the air. This procedure usually had the requisite effect of frightening them into surrender, but during the recent war years ammunition was scarce and accordingly I instructed my native rangers not to waste it by firing halting shots in such cases, with the result that many poachers evaded capture by running away into the bush.

The story then went round the local kraals that the native rangers had no ammunition at all, and that the rifles which they still carried were there just for show. Of course the poaching fraternity became increasingly bold and venturesome, penetrating a good deal further into the Park than they were wont to do previously. These poachers had to cross at least two fairly wide motor roads and in traversing these they would adopt the plan of walking backwards – taking care to leave a well-defined spoor on the road with the object of misleading any of my native rangers who might locate the spoor.

Now there was one particular gang of these poachers which was giving me a lot of trouble and proving themselves very difficult to catch. After a good deal of fruitless endeavour I hit upon the plan of collecting my native rangers from their respective pickets and sending them out on patrol from my own headquarters. The gang in question was operating in the neighbourhood of Pretorius Kop, but when the native rangers arrived there the poachers ceased their activities.

It then struck me that one of the native camp attendants then working in the rest camp might be in league with the poachers, and that very likely he had informed the latter of the movements

of the rangers, so I transferred the native rangers to an old deserted labourers' camp near the Shabine[13] koppie, ordering them to patrol from there and to avoid appearing near Pretorius Kop. Very early on the fourth morning while out on patrol my men struck the fresh spoor of nine poachers heading for Doispane's, and as it had rained during the previous night the spoor was easily followed.

For fifteen miles the spoor was trailed and on the way the policemen discovered where the poachers had killed a warthog, which they had cut up and taken along with them. Thence the tracks led towards a koppie with an overhanging rock which would provide shelter from the rain and where the poachers obviously intended to camp and make their hunting headquarters. As my rangers stealthily and quietly approached this koppie they presently noticed smoke from a fire issuing from beneath the overhanging rock. A very cautiously conducted advance nearer revealed the figures of nine natives sitting round the fire. One had a rifle in his hand and other rifles could be seen leaning up against the rock.

With one accord the rangers shouted, "We have caught you! Don't shoot! You are surrounded!" The poachers replied with a volley of shots, but none of my rangers were hit. The poachers were again called upon to surrender, but they were determined not to be caught and increased their fire. As of course my men disliked the idea of standing like dummies to be fired upon, they

---

[13] Shabeni

replied with two shots intended to frighten their opponents. Unfortunately one of the latter got hit and he died that night.

The remainder then surrendered and were arrested and they were found to have four rifles in their possession, the usual lot of assegais and six dogs. They were all finally tried and convicted in court. My native rangers were charged with murder, but I am glad to say they were eventually discharged as they were only performing their duty and defending themselves. This episode certainly served to stop poaching for a time.

Sometimes on moonlight nights poachers would cross the Park's boundary, accompanied as usual by dogs, and chase game – more especially waterbuck – into a pool of water, where they would kill them with assegais. Wire snares are also used a great deal, set in places where game go down to drink. When, in the course of their patrols, native rangers came across a dead buck in a snare, they would conceal themselves near the spot and wait for the return of the owner of the snare, when they would rush out and capture him.

Lions are frequently caught in snares also. This particularly occurs in the native reserves, where lions have been raiding stock. The snare is set near the kill and on his return during the second night the lion often gets caught, and is usually killed with assegais. Sometimes, however, the beast manages to break the snare, returning to the Park with part of it still fastened round its neck.

I have on several occasions seen lions with a wire round the neck, the place sometimes quite raw where it had eaten into the skin, and think such lions would be very nasty animals to approach. My attention was once attracted to a case of this kind, where the animal was in an exceedingly thin and emaciated condition, having an especially unpleasant sore on its neck. I shot it, as in any case it could not have survived long, and on examining its carcass found that the wire had eaten right into the flesh, thereby accounting for the desperate condition of the poor creature.

At another time, while skinning a lion which I had shot, we found that it had been caught some years previously in a snare. In this case the wire had cut right through the skin, which had completely healed and grown over it, so that there was no outward sign of any wire. This, incidentally, reminds me of a very curious injury to a lion which is worthy of record. I noticed this particular beast – a very fine big male lion in his prime – and it appeared to me that he was in poor condition and looked very sick and on this account I decided to shoot him in order to find out what was wrong.

Having done so I examined him carefully all over, but at first I could find no sign of any wound or wire snare. Then I opened his mouth and at once the cause of his appalling state was manifest, for wedged strongly between his upper teeth and across the palate was a piece of hard wood from the small, shrubby thorn tree known as sickle bush. Of course the poor brute had

been quite unable to eat and so he had been gradually dying of starvation. I cannot pretend to explain how that piece of wood became lodged so securely and fatally in the lion's mouth.

While on the subject of poachers, I may as well record a few more instances of our encounters with them. One day, while patrolling the Mbeyamede spruit with two of my native rangers, we found fresh tracks of two natives who were evidently hunting. We spoored these poachers for many miles as they, in turn, were following giraffe spoor. However, they evidently failed to catch up with the giraffe for presently their tracks revealed that they had given up the 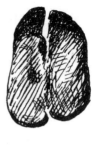 hunt and had turned aside after other game, and shortly after this we lost their spoor in some stony ground.

I felt certain that they must have a camp somewhere along the spruit, and we hoped to locate this at one of the many waterholes known to us along its course. Suddenly I noticed what seemed to be smoke curling up among the trees ahead of us, and my men having assured me that it was indeed smoke, we realised that we were close to the camp of the poachers.

Leaving my horse well concealed among the reeds of the spruit, we all crawled stealthily towards the smoke and presently we saw a native umfaan coming down to the waterhole with a calabash. We watched him fill this with water and retrace his steps and then we followed him, finding the camp close to the bank. It consisted of a shelter compound of chopped-down bushes with only one entrance. I advanced alone and rushed the gateway. Inside there were four natives, and two of these sprang through the leafy structure and got away, but the other two were caught and I knew that as long as I could catch even one we could find out who the others were.

The trees in and around the camp were festooned with meat of the game they had shot; some fresh and some already dry, and it was

clear that they had been operating pretty freely in this neighbourhood. By this time it was close to sundown and we had about eight miles to march before we reached our camp. My men begged me to allow them to tie up some of the meat and make the prisoners carry it back for them, so I told them to hurry as it would soon be dark and meanwhile went in search of my horse, which was still standing where I had left him.

Returning to the camp with the horse, I questioned the prisoners as to where they had hidden their rifles. They replied that they themselves had no rifles, merely, in fact, being there to collect the meat, but that the other two natives with the rifles were still out hunting but would be back any moment. They gave me the names of the men concerned and I knew them both; in fact, one of them used to be an old policeman of mine. While talking to the prisoners I suddenly caught a glimpse through the bush fence of a native approaching from the waterhole.

At first I thought it was one of my own followers returning from a drink, and it was not until the native had approached right up to the camp that I realised my mistake as I noticed then that he was carrying a rifle. Of course he was quite unaware of our presence until he reached the camp and observed me and my horse and then, in a flash, he withdrew his rifle from his shoulder, pointed it straight at me, and fired. Fortunately for myself, and no doubt greatly to his surprise, he missed me, and turning about he made a rush for the spruit.

As he was running away I thought to myself, "Well, you've had a shot at me so I'll take a shot at you in return!" He was a well-built, sturdy native, completely uncovered to the waist as he wore only an old impala skin *majoba* tied round his loins. As he ran away I put my sights in between his broad shoulder blades and pulled the trigger, but fortunately for him, and perhaps for me also, the cartridge cap snapped and his life was saved. I had fired hundreds of rounds through this old rifle and this was the first time I had had a misfire!

The only thing to do now was to pack up and trek homewards and we finally reached camp late that night, with our clothing severely torn by the thorn bush. We received all necessary information as to the proper identification of the other poachers from the prisoners and it was an easy matter to arrest them. Next day I gave my men permission to collect the remainder of the meat and I accompanied them back to the poachers' camp. We found that none of the others had returned to the camp. Afterwards, when finally caught, they informed me that they had travelled all night to get out of the Park and had only reached their kraals late next day. They were all tried and convicted. When the case was in court I refrained from charging the leader of the party with having fired at me as I thought we were quits to hang – had he shot me, or had I shot him!

Another old noted poacher was one Lomagando, who lived not far from the Park boundary. He was as black as the Devil's riding boots and I and my native rangers took several rifles from him at different times, but sooner or later he always managed to acquire another. These I knew he bought from poor whites in the district, but could never obtain proof. It is of course a very serious offence to sell rifles to natives, but Lomagando was always very loyal to the seller. He always told the same old tale: a white

man had come to his kraal with a rifle for sale and though he had bought it, he had never seen the white man since!

One day, after capturing him for the fourth time, I asked him what was to be the fitting end of his long career of repeated crime. After a little reflection he solemnly replied, "Nkosi, if a baboon is always stealing mealies in your land the only thing to do is to shoot it!"

Once when I caught him he had with him an old .303 rifle, with both .303 and Martini ammunition. I told him to hand over both rifles, but he assured me that he possessed only one – a .303. When I asked him what he was doing with the other cartridges he replied that he altered them to fit the .303. This I would not believe, so he suggested that if I would remove his handcuffs he would demonstrate. He then removed the lead bullet from the Martini-Henry cartridge and took out some of the powder.

"So far, so good," said I, "but what about the cap?" He asked me for a hammer and the old nut of a bolt and having been given these, he filled the cartridge case with water. He then walked up to a marula tree (which has a thick, soft bark) and placed the cartridge against the bark, holding the nut over the cap so as not to explode it, and gave it a hit with the hammer. The pressure from the water inside the cartridge case forced out the cap. He then did the same thing to the .303 and took the cap from the Martini-Henry and put it in the .303 case. He then hammered the Martini lead bullet on a tree to the correct size to fit the .303, cut a piece off it as it was too long, and then fitted it in the case. Proudly turning to me he said, "Nkosi, that is how I do it! If you like you can fire it!"

However, I very definitely preferred to watch him fire his home-made cartridge himself. He then fired at, and hit, a selected mark on a tree sixty yards from where we stood, and I was then quite convinced that he indeed had only one rifle.

Lomagando's last poaching trip – so far as I know at any rate – ended when he was arrested by N/R Mankoti, who was a very plucky native. Although it is the usual practice for native rangers to patrol in pairs, as it is dangerous work, Mankoti always preferred to carry out his patrols by himself – and later this preference of his cost him his life.

One day, during one of his solitary patrols, he heard the report of a rifle and on going to investigate he found Lomagando skinning a wildebeest which he had just shot. As this episode had taken place in quite open country and there were no trees or cover of any sort at that particular spot, Mankoti was seen long before he could get up to the poacher. However, he ran towards the latter and was fired at three times while so doing. Luckily the intrepid native ranger was not hit by any of these shots and he successfully arrested Lomagando, who was duly tried and convicted. On this occasion I told the prisoner that the next time he was caught poaching he would most certainly be shot. This threat so far seems to have had good results, though possibly he is now too old and has given up his bad habits.

As I have said previously, Mankoti's custom of patrolling alone finally cost him his life, and this is how it happened. One day, while on patrol, he happened to be in the vicinity of his father's kraal and he spent the night there. Early next morning he left his people to resume his duties. On the following day his father noticed vultures circling about some distance from his kraal and,

thinking that lions had made a kill and that there might be some meat to be had, he and his friends went to look. When they reached the scene they found a dead lion lying in a small open space with N/R Mankoti's rifle, tunic and hat covering it. Thence, after some time, they followed the blood spoor of Mankoti, whose dead body they finally found propped up against a tree in a sandy spruit some fifty yards or so away. A full and careful investigation of the signs suggested the following tragic drama.

The lion had evidently charged Mankoti, for what reason will never be known. As it rushed towards him, probably uttering the usual threatening choky growls, he fired at it, hitting it in the chest but not mortally, and in the next instant it caught hold of him. In the struggle that ensued Mankoti must have gamely pulled out his sheath knife and stabbed the lion again and again until he had succeeded in killing it. He himself had been very badly mauled, and he now found that he was too weak to walk. So having placed his belongings on the lion's body (possibly a final dramatic gesture), he crawled painfully to the little spruit where he knew that the sandy bed would hold some water, as fortunately it was the rainy season. He there scratched a hole in the sand and had a drink before crawling towards the tree against which he propped himself up — evidently dying there shortly afterwards.

Mankoti was an excellent native ranger with a very strong sense of duty, and I felt his loss very deeply.

## Chapter 10
# NOTES ON ANIMAL LIFE

During my patrols in the Game Reserve I had plenty of opportunities for observing interesting incidents in animal life, but unfortunately during those early days I neglected to keep regular personal notes of the many interesting things I saw and it is not always easy to remember them.

The pretty little saddle-backed jackals which are numerous over all the southern parts of the Kruger National Park prey largely upon small mammals; the eggs and young of ground-nesting birds; francolin and guineafowl when they can be successfully caught; and the young of the smaller buck. To this bill of fare they also add certain bush-fruits in season and various sorts of insects, while, as everybody knows, they depend greatly on the leavings from the kills of lions and other greater beasts of prey.

But that these jackals also occa-

sionally attack the young of the larger antelope was revealed to me when I once witnessed a jackal trying to catch a newly born blue wildebeest calf. Every time the jackal approached the calf the mother wildebeest, which was standing guard, would lower her head, her wild-looking eyes blazing with anger, and with a determined rush chase the small enemy away. Away would rush the jackal, very easily outpacing its infuriated pursuer. However, as soon as the latter returned to her offspring the jackal would approach once more, and evidently it hoped to tire out the cow wildebeest for this procedure was repeated for some while as I watched. Then, out of compassion for the anxious mother, I shot at the jackal, which then cleared off.

Blue wildebeest, unlike some other antelopes, do not hide their calves after they have been born, returning to the latter from time to time to feed them until they are old enough to join and run with the herd. The blue wildebeest cow, after it has dropped its calf, merely stands guard over the tiny, fawn-coated creature for an hour or two and after that brief period the little calf is strong enough to accompany its proud mother back to the troop, where it will run with the remainder.

The young of roan and sable antelope, waterbuck and smaller game such as reedbuck, duiker, etc. are not nearly so sturdily equipped by Nature; and I have often found newly born infants of these species lying carefully tucked up in a patch of grass or bush where their mothers had hidden them until they were strong enough to join the herd, a period in some cases extending to a week. I have often watched the moth-

er antelope very cautiously advance to where the calf is hidden, give it a drink, and stand there for a while, sniffing it and caressing its silky little coat with her tongue until the little wobbly legs become tired once more and the little beast sinks down in its form for the needful, strengthening slumber again. Then, after a final glance round to see that all is well (during which the air is well tested by the dilated, sensitive nostrils and the questioning alert ears query every sound), the mother very carefully and quietly moves away to graze a little way off in the bush until she knows that feeding time has again arrived.

Once my dogs, as they accompanied me, found a roan antelope calf, but, as is their custom with very young animals, they

did not bite it but merely held it down with their paws. I called them off and the little shaggy-coated calf with its long, rather donkey-like tufted ears, groggily walked up to my horse, which it evidently mistook for its mother. It nosed questioningly about the horse as if it wanted a drink, meanwhile uttering a funny sort of whistling noise.

It was not long before I heard a rustle in the grass behind me, and on looking round I saw that the mother roan was approaching at no great distance. I now pushed the little calf gently in front of me until I had guided it close to its mother, who was standing in a very threatening attitude, tossing her head vigorously and snorting angrily, and then quickly ran back so that the calf could not follow me. The mother now stepped briskly up to her offspring and sniffed it all over, rather suspiciously at first, as it no doubt still retained traces of the combined scents of human and dog, before trotting off into the bush with the calf following her.

Although there are plenty of lions inhabiting the Kruger National Park, it is extremely rare that cases of deliberate attacks upon human beings (with the object of devouring them) have been recorded by, or brought to the notice of, the staff. This of course is mainly because the average lion so naturally dislikes and distrusts human beings – seeming to have an instinctive fear of them, probably instilled through many centuries during which man has been the one aggressive and dangerous enemy – that it hesitates, under normal conditions where there is plenty of its natural prey about, even to eat a man's flesh after it has killed him in self-defence.

If, however, a lion becomes incapacitated through injury and is unable to catch his ordinary prey, or when driven by hunger through old age and weakness, the desperate urge of famine may prompt him to pounce on a solitary human being, his more cautious instincts subdued by the primary craving for food. Ever afterwards he will continue to hunt man, both because he has now overcome that instinctive distrust and fear and because he now finds that the "Lord of Creation" is a good deal safer and easier to catch than any wild animal, being stupid in comparison with the lower beasts so far as looking after himself in the bush in question. He discovers, in fact, that – so far as the use of his natural senses is concerned at any rate – the "iron colossus" has feet of clay!

There is no doubt though that, as in the case of most wild creatures, instinct itself is rarely sufficient unless well driven home by parental example and training; and this may be observed where young wild animals are captured when very small. Young lions and leopards very often take naturally to their owners, displaying no instinctive fear, and young lions and young buck often become quite friendly together. To this extent young, inexperienced lions in the wild state may prove more liable to attack human beings under certain conditions than more mature beasts – if only from motives of curiosity or experiment. Although such an attack might be more accidental than deliberate, should it result in the beast actually devouring its victim, only its subsequent destruction will prevent it from becoming a dangerous maneater.

While on my way to Skukuza one day to interview the warden, I was halted in the road by a native who appeared to be very excited. He informed me that his old mother had been killed and eaten by lions during the night, but as my business with the warden was of a very urgent nature I was unable to look into the matter just then and it was not till after nightfall that I eventually returned home. Next morning, however, I visited the kraal and was promptly informed by its agitated inhabitants that the lions had returned during the night and had endeavoured to force their way into a hut in which a young girl was sleeping.

The old woman who had been killed during the previous night had apparently occupied a hut in company with a little granddaughter aged about ten years. Next morning when the girl got up she found that her old granny was absent, but she felt no concern at this at first, merely thinking that the old lady had risen earlier than she herself in order to attend to her various domestic duties. Shortly after this her father entered the hut and asked where the old woman was. On investigating it was found that nobody had seen or heard her go away and, everybody now distinctly alarmed, a search in the near vicinity was begun. Not very far away in the bush the horror-stricken relatives discovered the battered remains of the old woman's head and one leg bone: all that was left of her mortal remains.

From a study of the available traces it was learn that, during the night, the old lady must have gone outside her hut and in doing so must have walked right into two lions which happened to be close to the door. They must have killed her at once before she had time to cry out, because nobody in the kraal had heard the slightest sound. The two lions had then dragged her a short way off and completely devoured her with the exception of the two fragments described above. These tragic remains were buried by her son.

In this case, as usual, the lions, having tasted human flesh, lost their fear of man. They returned nightly to the kraal, catching and killing all the goats and fowls. At first I thought they were probably old lions which could not kill game any longer and of course I hunted them until I finally got them both. I was surprised to discover that they were two young lions not yet in their prime; and I feel sure that the reason why they killed the old woman in the first place was because, in coming out of her hut, she had blundered right into them.

In their excitement, and having tasted her blood, they began to eat her and evidently found this new dish highly satisfactory. At any rate, had they not been accounted for as soon as possible these two would no doubt have become exceedingly dangerous animals. I am convinced that these two were indeed the culprits, for from the moment of their deaths there was no further trouble at that or neighbouring kraals.

While on the subject of lions, I would like to add that they are great bluffers. I feel sure that a lot of other lion hunters will agree with me on this point, though this does not hold good of leopards which, once they have made up their minds to charge, cannot be stopped except by a well-placed bullet.

Of course it is proverbially unwise to generalise about the lion, and while there is probably no more dangerous animal in the world when thoroughly aroused, some individual lions will put up with a great deal of annoyance without wholeheartedly taking the offensive, as the following incident will show.

We were following two lions which had been killing a lot of stock belonging to natives then living in the game reserve. It was a very hot day and we had followed them for some miles, frequently disturbing them, but they always managed to elude me before I could get in a shot. Now, lions do not like being disturbed constantly, especially on a hot day, as they dislike power-

ful sun and prefer to seek cool, shady retreats where they can sleep in peace. They are more apt to become bad-tempered through disturbance under such conditions.

In fact, on this occasion, while we were pushing through a patch of long, rank tamboekie grass, one of the lions demonstrated his increasing annoyance by standing in the long grass, growling very wickedly and presently making a couple of short rushes towards us. His movements were evident from the swishing and moving of the grass and the threatening grunts and growls, as the herbage was so tall that I was unable to see the lion himself. Apparently this demonstration was merely to cover his retreat, for he presently ran off through the grass in the opposite direction.

The next time we came up with them the lions were in a patch of grass in a donga, and as we had cut the spoor all round in the bush and saw none coming out of the donga, I knew they were still there. I told one of the men to throw stones into the patch,

and the arrival of the second stone was promptly greeted by a terrific roar while the grass at our end of the donga began to sway violently, indicating that the lion was again charging towards us. In fact, the demonstration was so menacing, and the accompanying sounds so awe-inspiring, that it proved too much for my men, who hastily ran backwards and stood.

I am ashamed to confess that I myself did likewise, though mainly in order to get a clear view in case there was a chance for a shot. But although quite obviously by now in a thoroughly furious rage, the lion still did not press his charge home; only coming to the edge of the grass before turning once more, and presently both of them broke out on the further side of the patch and made off again before we could catch a satisfactory glimpse of them.

As it was now just about sundown, and we were many miles from home, I had to give up the hunt, finally reaching M'timba about 10 p.m. – tired, hungry and disappointed; but that is one of the things a lion hunter has to put up with!

Lions are very intelligent animals, as I have proved many times while hunting them. One day, along the Sabi, I found fresh spoor of a very big lion and, after following his tracks for some distance, we put him up but failed to get in a shot. We traced him for a long distance and his spoor would lead on for some two or three miles before the traces revealed that he had lain down when, getting our wind, he would jump up with a growl and trot along further. Later on we disturbed him near a troop of blue wildebeest which, when they sighted us, began to snort in their usual manner. Away went our lion once more, presently lying up close to another troop of blue wildebeest, which in their turn warned him of our approach by snorting when they caught sight of us.

This clever manoeuvre was repeated four times, the lion always electing to rest near a herd of wildebeest, which invariably gave the alarm. Eventually he managed to elude us altogether and we had to leave him as he had proved himself to be too clever for us. I am certain that this lion deliberately selected the company of the wildebeest, and that it was not through mere coincidence that we disturbed him close to four troops of wildebeest on four separate occasions.

Natives have certain superstitious customs in connection with hunting, and one of the most important of these is never to point with the index finger to the spoor of lions, or at game, in the manner usual with Europeans. Natives always point with their thumb on these occasions; and after years of hunting with them, as I used to do, I found that I had unconsciously adopted the same habit myself.

The spotted hyena is a curious animal – in fact, I think it is the weirdest of all the animals in the Kruger National Park. No wonder that the older natives believe that the *amatagati* (witches) can change themselves into hyenas, prowling about in the dead of night and bewitching people.

Some tribes assert that the witches (who are held to be very numerous among native communities) use hyenas as their special steeds, riding about on them at night while pursuing their nefarious affairs. One has only to listen to that weird, ghostly moaning howl, "Auuuuu-ee!" as it rises and falls quaveringly and mysteriously in the dimness of the bush beyond one's campfire at night to realise how pregnant with horror it must have been to the superstitious inhabitants of the kraals in days gone by.

Hyenas, of course, are not particular as to what they eat, their diet ranging from human corpses to old discarded shoes. Unlike most carnivores they usually hide what portion of a meal they cannot eat at once.

One day I was resting under a big tree at the 'Mbeamede[14] Spruit, near a small pool of water about 18 inches deep. Suddenly I saw a hyena trotting down the bank, carrying something in his mouth. He advanced to the pool and dropped what he was carrying into the water, and then stood back to watch the effects of his action. Apparently he was astonished and dissatisfied with the fact that the piece of meat (or whatever it was) floated on the surface, for presently he entered the water, seized the meat in his mouth and pushed it below the surface once more. It promptly rose and floated again, and this seemed to cause the hyena a great deal of concern.

I could almost imagine that I saw the expression of astonishment in his face. His expression, in fact, was so ludicrous that I was unable to control a chuckle and this startled him, so that he glanced nervously in my direction before ambling off. I waited a while, but as he did not return I went down to the pool to find out what the object was that he evidently valued so highly. It turned out to be a fragment of lung of either wildebeest or waterbuck and of course, being light and buoyant, it naturally floated

---

[14] Mbyamiti Spruit

near the surface of the water. On scratching round the bottom of the pool I found some decomposed bones, which proved that this unusual place was evidently his larder for the lean times!

Hyenas are a curious mixture of cowardice and audacity. They will often dash right into the middle of a camp when all is quiet and the inhabitants asleep and grab hold of and make off with anything they can find, even an old bone or a piece of skin that no other animal will eat.

Once during the Boer War, while on my duties of patrolling and inspecting the various pickets along the Lebombo towards the Olifants, I shot a very fine sable antelope, whose head I wanted for my collection. Since it was too late to bring the head and meat into my small camp, and as I had two men with me and it was a warm night, I decided to camp on the spot. We had no blankets and we just lay on the ground. I cut off the sable's head and placed it near our fire, around which we slept all night. During the night, while we slept, a hyena came along, leapt over one of the sleeping natives, seized the sable head and made off with it. We found the horns next morning, but the head was completely spoilt.

Why the hyena took the head from alongside the fire, instead

of going to the carcass which was only a couple of hundred yards away, I leave to a wiser head than mine to explain!

Incidentally, and as a matter of curious interest, the tails of hyenas are greatly prized by witch doctors and the latter will pay quite high prices for them.

The full-throated roar of a lion, when heard at close quarters when he is really letting go, is a most awe-inspiring and grand sound. The atmosphere vibrates with the immense volume and harsh resonance of the roars, and when several lions are calling in unison, each taking up the chorus in turn, the effect is indescribable. I have known some of my best lion-hunting dogs to be subdued into complete silence when a lion is roaring very loudly and when he is very close to camp; although when he has made off and is still roaring at a little distance, they will renew their excited barking.

Many years ago, when camped on the Olifants River, I was unable to sleep one night as the result of a long previous day's march together with the approach of a dose of malaria. As I lay restlessly tossing in my blankets I heard a party of lions roaring about two miles away up the river, and presently another party seemed to reply from about a similar distance down the river. The two prides were mutually approaching; and when they arrived within hearing distance of one another it appeared as if each pride was attempting to outroar the other.

Eventually they met quite close to my camp (it took about two hours or more before the actual contact was made), and then the noise created seemed to shake the ground and the walls of my little hut vibrated. Each crescendo of cavernous roars would terminate

in the usual series of loitering husky and grating grunts, but before these had died away to final drawn-out sighs the opposing chorus would drown the epilogue. So it went on, until finally the combined excitement seemed to flare up into a fight between the two prides, after which I suppose each one continued its own direction, for a little later I heard them roaring in the distance – one lot up the river and the other downstream.

In all my experience I have never heard lions so noisy before or since. I would greatly have liked to visit the battlefield next day, as in a fight like that lions are very often killed or at least seriously mauled, but by then fever had me in its grip and I was unable to go.

I have on several occasions found lions which had been killed in a fight, or have shot them when they had been so badly mauled that they would never have recovered. One morning when I was later living at Pretorius Kop, I happened to be at M'timba when the postman, who carried the post from Pretorius Kop to White River by cycle, arrived in a very excited state.

He said that he had been chased by a lion as he was pedalling along the road about two miles from Pretorius Kop camp. He stated that he had come across two lions lying by the side of the road and that, as there was no chance of turning back, he had simply carried on with his bicycle, hoping that the lions would not chase him. However, one lion jumped up and chased him for quite a

distance, increasing his alarm considerably by grunting ominously as it did so. Fortunately for him the road surface at this point was hard and good and he also happened to have a long downhill slope ahead of him, so that he succeeded in outpacing his pursuer.

This particular native was born and bred in the lion country and I knew that he had had good cause for his fright, and as I still had one old rifle left at the old home I took it with me in case I saw the lion on my return journey. The man explained to me the place where the incident had occurred.

In due course I reached the spot and got out of my car to examine the spoor on the road. There was his bicycle track with the spoor of the lion covering it, and it was clear that the lion had been running all out as his footprints had torn up the ground. On driving on a little further I saw the two lions lying a little way off the road. One of them looked quite nasty and, knowing that he was the culprit, I got out of my car to see what he would do. He at once came straight for me, so I shot him, and on examining his body found that he had recently been badly bitten in a fight. This no doubt accounted for his bad temper.

I would like here to emphasise, as a result of my long experience of the habits and behaviour of lions, that there is very good ground for the warning to tourists in the Kruger National Park to remain in their cars and not to get out and approach animals in

order to get a better view, or sometimes merely to show off. This warning does not seem to be taken seriously enough and very often it is merely regarded as a silly piece of official nonsense. Sooner or later there is bound to occur a very serious accident to those who ignore this advice, and then it will be too late to be sorry. In fact, I am surprised that this has not happened already.

At one time we used to get our milk from M'timba, carried by a native on a bicycle; and although it was a long distance (eleven miles each way) we did not like to do without it. For a while all went well: the umfaan riding the bicycle always arriving in good time, though he often reported seeing lions en route. But one day he was late, and on his arrival he was very upset and said that he had been chased by two lions, and refused to carry on with the job. However, I hired another umfaan who expressed his willingness to undertake the task. Three days later he also reported the same thing and also refused to continue, so I loaded him into my car and told him to show me the spot where he had been chased, taking with me a shotgun loaded with No. 6 shot. Sure enough, the lions were still there – two young males. I got out of the car and peppered them with the No. 6, sending them grunting off into the bush, and they never interfered with the milkman again after this salutary lesson.

In due course the old bicycle became worn out and as new supplies were unobtainable during the war period, our milk supply from M'timba had to be stopped.

The question as to whether animals possess a "sixth sense" or not has ever been a fruitful source of argument and, for my own part, my personal experience of wild animals, especially lions, inclines me strongly to the view that they do indeed possess such a sense that serves to warn them of danger, etc., and this has nothing to do with sight, scent or hearing.

One morning I was travelling by car along the twelve-mile circular route close to Pretorius Kop when I came across five lionesses setting upon a wildebeest which they had pulled down. That they had only just secured their prey was evident from the fact that the wildebeest was not yet entirely dead; still giving a convulsive kick now and again though it was obviously on the very point of expiring. As I arrived and halted my car to watch the scene at the kill (which was only ten yards off the road, in open bush) the lionesses began to tear away voraciously at the wildebeest, uttering the usual gurgling growls and grunts audible at such occasions.

They were just beginning to get at the meat when I saw one lioness pause, flatten her ears, and glance fixedly in the direction of some trees about one hundred yards away. She then left the wildebeest and slunk off, passing just behind my car before vanishing from my view in the long grass. After her came the other four lionesses, all of them doing the same thing, and I was greatly puzzled at their behaviour.

All of a sudden the cause of the lionesses' curious behaviour was explained for, from the shade of the trees – towards which the lionesses had glanced in their first alarm – appeared a big male lion, closely followed by four others of the same sex. With swaggering confidence and masculine self-assurance the five

gentlemen strolled carelessly up to the dead wildebeest and took possession of it, and their behaviour was not disputed by the lionesses, which made no further appearance.

Now, how did those lionesses learn about the approach of the lions? They certainly could not see the latter, and I do not think that they could hear them. Moreover, why did those lionesses abandon all rights to their kill to the lions, hastily retreating, in fact, as if on account of some serious breach of leonine etiquette? It all goes to prove that many things happen in the veld which man cannot account for.

A few years ago a professor and his wife from overseas were visiting the Park. It so happened that they struck the rainy season, and while crossing one of the spruits about seven miles from Pretorius Kop the car stalled.

The spruit came down in torrent while they were still in this predicament, lifting the car bodily and bearing it downstream. The professor just had time to grab his coat, in which he had his money in notes, and assist his wife to get out of the rapidly rising stream. By this time it was nearly sundown and the benighted pair had to set out towards camp on foot.

When his car had stalled in the stream the professor had removed his shoes and socks, which had subsequently been lost

with his car, and the resulting fact that he had to go barefoot over the gravelly ground increased the unpleasantness of this enforced march through lion country in the gathering gloom.

Meanwhile the camp superintendent had sent me a message to say that this particular party had failed to return to camp, and he thought that they must be stranded in some spruit. I sent out my lorry with a search party to look for them: no simple matter as nobody had any idea which road they had taken. However, eventually the missing couple were located – up a tree!

According to the professor, all went well for the first part of their rather nerve-racking journey towards the camp in the dusk on foot. But within about two miles of home they came upon five lions lying in the road and they hurriedly climbed into the nearest tree. One can imagine their anxiety and distress: they had walked about four or five miles in the increasing darkness and they had to do this barefoot since, as mentioned above, their shoes had been washed off the running board of the car. In addition to this both of them were wet, cold and weary. Only shortly out from England, they were unused to roughing it, let alone wandering about wild country inhabited by savage beasts!

Then their worst fears were confirmed and they came on to the lions. It is not difficult to picture the worthy professor anxiously assisting his terrified wife into the nearest available tree: his determined efforts to assist her high enough with the minimum of time wasted being accelerated by his own sense of urgency. Meanwhile, possibly, the lions, their interest awakened by the strange scene being enacted not far from them, silently debated among themselves whether a nearer investigation might prove worthwhile!

Anyhow, they successfully settled themselves in the tree and spent a little while there, praying devoutly that a search party would be sent to look for them. Suddenly their hopes were raised by the gleam of light from a lorry, almost immediately to be dashed again as the lorry apparently turned off along another route. However, presently it reappeared, evidently having negotiated a bend in the road, and as it approached nearer the professor and his wife shouted loudly and desperately. They were successful in attracting attention and were duly rescued and brought back to camp, where they were provided with dry clothes.

Next day the professor's bank notes had to be ironed out between blotting paper, as they were saturated. I accompanied him and his wife back to the spruit where they had lost their car and we found it about one hundred yards downstream, half buried in sand. After a lot of trouble it was dug out and towed back to camp. This little tale will emphasise the wisdom of the

Park authorities in closing the Park during the rainy season, quite apart from considerations of malaria.

I will conclude this chapter with a rather remarkable incident which I think is worth recording.

I was travelling by lorry one day when I noticed a wildebeest flat on its side, apparently dead. I drove up to within a few feet of the recumbent animal and told the men to load it into the lorry and we would take it home as meat for the camp. The men now sprang off the lorry and stood round the wildebeest, and I asked them what had killed it. They replied that, so far as they could see; there were no signs of snakebite, nor could they see any marks on the body, but intimated to me that they would turn it over and examine its lower side.

One man got hold of the front legs and another the hind ones, but just as they were about to haul it over that wildebeest suddenly came to life! With a grunt of alarm it leapt to its feet (to the general startled scattering of the natives) and without further ado it bolted into the bush. Apparently it had merely been fast asleep, but in all my experience I have never known game to sleep so soundly.

CHAPTER 11

# WILD PETS

At one period, during the early days of the old game reserve, there was a great deal of rumour about buried treasure in some mysterious part of the Lowveld. This treasure was popularly known as the "Kruger Millions", and the tale went that, round about 1900, the Republican Government treasure had been buried for safety against the hazards of war in some remote part of what was then the Sabi Game Reserve.

We were constantly badgered by treasure-seeking parties of greater or lesser degree and we naturally kept our own eyes open to any interesting-sounding discoveries in our particular areas of the reserve.

One evening at sundown I was just dismounting from my horse after a long patrol when one of my men approached me in a very mysterious manner. Having evidently satisfied himself that there was nobody else within earshot, he excitedly informed me that he had, that morning, discovered some natives digging a big hole in the bush about six miles away from my camp. When they noticed him the natives ran away, and my informant went to examine the excavation. He found a big flat box which they had unearthed still lying at the bottom of the hole.

Needless to say, my mind at once leapt to the Kruger Millions and I ordered the man to take with him a companion and their greatcoats, and to mount guard over that spot all night, promising that I would be there first thing in the morning. I then settled down to a restless, deliriously excited and sleepless night, reflecting joyfully what I would do with all the wealth shortly to be at my disposal!

I could hardly wait for the dawn and was soon at the spot. My disappointment may easily be judged, however, when, instead of seeing the big black box full of bars of gold which I had anticipated, all we found was a slab of slate. This, on examination, proved to be the headstone of some unknown person's grave, which had been undermined and had fallen into the hole. The name had merely been scratched on the slate and was well-nigh obliterated by weathering, and I have no doubt that the natives who had been digging there also had some notions of buried treasure. Very sadly, but a good deal wiser, we filled in the hole and set up the headstone once more, and for aught I know it remains there to this day.

Shortly after this it befell me to accompany several treasure-seeking parties in the reserve on different occasions. They always had a guide with them who, shortly after the Boer War, had "seen a tree with marks and crosses on it, and a mound of earth below it", but no treasure was ever found.

One party even came all the way up from the Cape, well fitted out with two mule wagons, beautiful riding horses, big tents and every luxury and comfort; but they, like the rest, went back empty-handed.

At different times I have kept wild animals as pets and found them an interesting study, though I have seldom kept them for long. A rather unusual pet was an Australian wild dog – known as a dingo – which was given to me as a two-month-old pup. He soon became quite at home with my own dogs, feeding out of the same trough with them, and he used to follow me all over the place. I could never persuade him to accompany my pack when I rode into the veld with them, which was just as well perhaps.

All went well for a time, and then his wild nature asserted itself and he began to kill the fowls. I tried to train him otherwise, but it was never any use, and in the end he had to be destroyed. I had two Alsatian pups that developed the same failing. They were very cunning and took no notice of fowls during the day, no matter how close the latter might stray, but Heaven help the misguided fowl that slept within their reach at night! I eventually sent them to my farm, where they proved to be excellent at herding cattle.

Another of my unusual pets was a bush pig, which I caught when it was about six weeks old. It was an intelligent little creature and soon it became quite tame, living with my dogs, whose porridge and milk it used to share in the same trough

when it grew older. My sisters with their children habitually spent the winter months with me and very often, as the children were playing in the yard, the bush pig would appear. I suppose the somewhat uncouth, bristly appearance of the  wild pig scared the children, for as a rule they would rush away with screams of terror and this, of course, alarmed their mothers, so that a great hubbub would ensue.

Sometimes a child would fall in its haste and the pig would trot up to it, stand contemplating it comically for a while, and then run away. In fact it showed evidence in many ways of a strong sense of humour, and it never made any attempt to hurt or interfere with the children.

I have tried to tame warthog, of which I have caught several small ones, but never successfully. They either always escaped from the pen in which they were confined, or else refused to eat or drink and so died.

One of the various lion cubs I have kept for longer or shorter periods was caught near Doispane's, after I had shot the mother. This cub was about two months old and it fought like a little demon until my men managed to strap it to a pole by means of the halter riems from my horse. In this manner, securely trussed up, it was carried to camp by two men.

For quite a few days the little beast remained very savage and suspicious, cowering back when approached and growling and spitting as savagely as any adult lion in like circumstances; the lights of terror and hate glowing from its large eyes as it rolled them from side to side, revealing the whites, while it guardedly watched every angle of one's advance. By degrees, however, hunger got the better of it, and with careful and patient handling

it eventually was coaxed to take some food, and after that it became quite tame.

I took this cub to M'timba, where I had some pups of about the same age, and the little creature took to them very easily and they all became exceedingly friendly and romped together quite contentedly.

As the pups grew older they started to hunt about in the neighbouring bush on their own account and the young lion accompanied them; so, fearing that it would escape altogether, I chained it up. A few nights later it managed to slip its chain, and it immediately set out after the dogs, dragging the chain.

When the dogs returned on the following morning no lion accompanied them and, feeling very anxious as to its fate, I sent out a search party in search of the little miscreant. However, in spite of repeated and careful hunting we were unable to trace it, and after about a week we gave it up, reluctantly assuming that its chain had become entangled in the bush and that it had, as a result, died of starvation.

And then, one morning at dawn, I heard a catlike mewing outside my bedroom window and on looking out saw the lion cub. It was in a pitiful condition as a result of its week's absence in the bush, a mere bag of skin and bone; and it is a remarkable fact that it had survived at all. From then on it became very docile and good-tempered and became a general favourite, appearing especially fond of my son, whose pet it really was.

Unfortunately, as it grew larger the question of providing adequate food became a steadily increasing problem. Porridge and milk were no longer suitable and it now required meat every day and in steadily increasing quantity, and this, in our particular circumstances, was not always procurable. We hated to part with so interesting and attractive a little beast, but in the end I gave it to the late Hon. P.G.W. Grobler, who was then Minister of Lands and who had played so great a part in achieving the successful passage of the National Parks Bill through the Union Parliament in 1926. Though he enthusiastically received this gift of the lion cub, Mr Grobler also in due course found its maintenance rather a problem, and so he in turn presented it to the Johannesburg Zoo.

At least a year after its arrival we happened to be up in Johannesburg, and as usual we visited the zoo. When we reached the lion's cage it was feeding time and our young lioness was at the far end, engrossed in a bone which she was chewing. My son Henry recognised her by a scar she had on her nose and he called to her by her name – Elizabeth.

To his delight she immediately recognised his voice, looking up instantly and leaving her bone she came over to the bars of her cage and stood rubbing her head against them, indicating her obvious delight in this reunion! We were all greatly impressed at her quick recognition after more than a year's absence, and I think this little incident indicates the high degree of intelligence in lions, while it also proves that they have good memories.

At one time I used to employ some of my leisure hours in doing a little taxidermy work – preserving and mounting the heads and skins of buck, lions, leopards, etc. – and as this was often a rather messy undertaking my wife, after many complaints about my dirty clothes, made me an apron out of white duck. Little did she realise that this apron would possibly later be instrumental in saving my life, and yet that this proved to be the case I think the following incident will show.

I was engaged one morning in taxidermy when one of the natives asked me to operate on a bull which he had brought for the purpose. I told him to throw the bull and I would come when they were ready. As my work was still unfinished I went to the kraal still wearing my apron, and when the operation was complete I told the men to loosen the riems with which the bull was tied, and turned away towards an opening in the kraal fence.

Hardly had I done so when, to the accompaniment of urgent cries to "look out", I heard a clattering of hooves behind me, rather emphasised by unpleasant ferocious snorts. Hastily glancing round I beheld the infuriated bull curvetting and prancing with undue speed in my direction. Within seconds he had arrived within a few feet and, whether as a result of instinct or despair I cannot tell, I hastily placed both my hands under the apron (as I had seen farm women do to chase away fowls and geese), and flipped it towards the fiery oncoming monster for all I was worth.

Fortunately this proved to be something with which the furious but limited brain of the bull was unable to cope, for he came to a dead stop, regarded the flapping white object with obvious bewilderment, and then turned about and charged my men with renewed vigour, sending them scattering wildly and noisily through the gateway and so into the veld. It finally fell to a little herdboy of about seven years to turn the bull, drive him quietly to the other cattle, and so bring him home.

Among my native rangers was a really fine native whose name was Forage Ngomane. He was a Shangaan and though he was born in the

Transvaal, he said that his parents originally came from Portuguese East Africa. Forage was of a very cheerful disposition and he incessantly joked with the other natives, invariably whistling at his work in camp or veld. He had only one serious fault – an undue devotion to the beer pots. In fact, the other natives used to complain that when the beer calabash was handed round the individual whose turn came next to Forage had to wait a very long time for a very small available quantity.

Forage was very keen on his police work and he made a first class detective. If I put him on a case he usually saw it through, and he had an almost uncanny sense of reading his fellow Africans' minds.

One day we were patrolling along the Sigaas River on horseback when we heard a rifle shot not far away. We promptly made for the place and discovered a freshly killed waterbuck, its carcass still warm. On looking round we found the footprints of a native leading towards the native reserve. We followed the tracks for some distance, but as a result of the dryness and hardness of the ground we finally lost them, then, on casting around, we suddenly came upon a native hoeing his land and we questioned him. First of all he denied having heard the shot, but after a little cross-questioning he finally admitted that he had done so, but had been afraid to approach the river in case he himself might be fired at by the poacher.

His evidence was given very clearly and smilingly and although I prided myself on being able to read the native mind – being able to speak their language quite fluently and, having grown up among them, being fairly conversant with their ways – I

quite believed what this native said, and the sight of him hoeing his land convinced me that he had nothing to do with the killing of the waterbuck.

Not so Forage, however! He took me aside and said, "Nkosi, that native either shot that waterbuck or knows who did so. Let me arrest him." So, to his voluble indignation and with many horrified protestations of his innocence, the native was arrested and informed that he would be charged with shooting the waterbuck.

We took him with us to where we were encamped and I sent back some of the men for the meat of the waterbuck. Next day we subjected our prisoner to a severe cross-examination. For a long time he obstinately stuck to his story, but finally he broke down and confessed that he had shot the waterbuck, and having done so was on his way back to his kraal to call his womenfolk to help carry the meat when he saw us in the distance approaching on horseback. He hid his rifle in the bush (this he handed in later) and made for his land, where he began to hoe with the object of putting us off the scent. Later he was convicted in court, and when I asked Forage how he realised the man was guilty, he replied that he could see it in his eyes.

Very often, when natives suspected of poaching or any other crime were brought in by my men and they had not too clear a case, I would hand the matter over to Forage. He seemed to be able to determine, within a very short while, whether the accused was guilty or not, and after a few hours of Forage's particular brand of cross-questioning the prisoner usually admitted his guilt.

Forage was as resourceful during his patrols in the veld as he was when cross-questioning a prisoner. As I have already men-

tioned, it was the usual procedure for my native rangers to patrol in pairs since there is a certain amount of danger associated with their work: from either wild animals, snake bite or poachers. During one of these patrols Forage's half-section, being subordinate to him, asked Forage to allow him to visit his kraal, which was close to where they were passing, arranging with him to meet him at a certain spot later in the day.

Forage continued his patrol alone and presently he observed the spoor of a gang of poachers, which he followed until he located their camp. He boldly walked right among them and, with his usual careless laugh, said: "Give me some of what you are eating!" The poachers (all of whom were known to Forage) were so taken aback at his audacity that they merely gaped at him and handed over two rifles in obedience to his demand. Somewhat recovering their composure, they then insolently declared that they would not permit Forage to arrest them as he was quite alone. To this Forage replied casually that the other rangers would arrive any moment, ordering his prisoners curtly to pack up their belongings. He then marched them back to my camp, having first taken the precaution to remove the bolt from each rifle and hide them in the veld.

This, I feel sure you will agree, was a pretty good effort on the part of Forage, as the poachers could easily have done away with him and no one would have been any the wiser.

As I have previously mentioned, Forage Ngomane's one weakness was his devotion to beer. One evening I said to him, "At four o'clock tomorrow morning you must see that my cart is inspanned and come with me on patrol across the Sand River." Sure

enough, at four o'clock on the following morning he had the cart ready. It was still fairly dark and I learnt afterwards that he had borrowed the assistance of two other men. I got into the Cape cart, took the reins and drove off with Forage sitting beside me. After a little way I noticed he was continually bumping up against me, but at first thought it was merely on account of the jolting of the cart. But, further on when it became light, I looked at him and then noticed that he was very drunk.

When we reached the Sand River, which had about three feet of water in it, I ordered him to get down and attend to the harness of one of the horses. He did so, but in such a clumsy, blundering way that I lost patience and, whipping up the horses, galloped through the river. Forage shouted to me to stop, but I shortly ordered him to jump into the water and come. With his usual obedience he came, but when he had reached midstream he stumbled and fell flat on his face in the water. Eventually he reached the bank, but the icy cold bath had sobered him and I waited for him to wring out his sopping clothes and then to clamber up beside me again, and off we went.

Forage was always most truthful. The only time he ever lied to me was once when I accused him of being drunk, and he replied, "Nkosi, I have had nothing to drink!" But a slight deviation from the truth on such occasions is by no means rare among white as well as black!

After about twenty years' excellent service Forage became ill. He developed a nasty cough and, though I tried all the available remedies, he made no progress. I then had him medically examined and the doctor's verdict was tuberculosis, and Forage was advised to go to a sanatorium for treatment. This he absolutely refused to do, saying that if he must die he would die in his home.

He kept on getting worse and as he could no longer perform his duties as a native ranger, I sent him to my farm where he could keep an eye on things for me and would have to do no work. I continued to pay him the salary he had been earning and, as the doctor said he must have nourishing food, he was allowed all the milk, cream and eggs on the farm. In spite of this his condition steadily deteriorated, until one New Year's morning one of my farm natives came to report that poor old Forage had passed away. I at once went over and saw that his remains were taken away and buried at his kraal as his womenfolk insisted. He was a stout fellow, with a splendid record.

Two of my native rangers, Helfas and Sokis, were on patrol near Ship Mountain. They heard a shot and on investigating they found two natives skinning a kudu bull which they had shot. As my men approached to arrest them, one of the poachers grabbed his rifle and fired point-blank at Helfas – fortunately missing him, though the bullet must have passed very close. Helfas then grappled with his assailant and Sokis chased the other, who ran off into the bush.

The poacher was a big, muscular native. Determined to resist arrest, he pulled out a knife and tried to stab Helfas, who jerked up his arm with the result that the blade only gashed the side of his face. He succeeded in knocking the knife out of the poacher's hand and then followed a struggle – Helfas meanwhile shouting to Sokis to come to his assistance, but the latter was by now too far off, chasing the other poacher, to hear him. Finally the poacher got Helfas by the throat and tried to throttle him. Helfas said later that everything turned black and he thought that his last moment had come, so he pulled out his sheath knife and stabbed his assailant in the arm, puncturing the biceps. He relaxed his hold on Helfas and, as several arteries had been severed, he soon expired.

I was out on patrol at the time and I met the two rangers coming to report. Helfas's face and head were wrapped up in a dirty old puttee, which was already soaked with blood. Having reached the scene of his struggle, I found that the dead poacher had been temporarily buried so that the wild animals could not get at him before the district surgeon came to hold a post-mortem.

Helfas was of course arrested and tried for manslaughter, but was discharged. He is a strapping big native and he has done excellent service, quite often having successfully arrested poachers who had defied other members of the staff. He has on three occasions arrested a native, Mazweni, who lives in Crown lands on the north bank of the Sabi. A very powerfully built man, Mazweni stands six feet six inches, all of it hard muscle. He never pays taxes to the government and he seems to have the gift of being able to induce any dog to follow him. He collects dogs from native kraals and crosses over into the Park with them to hunt game, especially warthog. Of course, he usually finds two or three other natives to accompany him.

The first time Helfas caught Mazweni they had a struggle and Helfas knocked Mazweni's legs from under him, and before he could recover he found himself securely handcuffed. After that, Mazweni would give himself up to Helfas, but to none other.

Once, after Mazweni had killed a sable antelope on a farm outside the Park, he was on his way home, carrying the meat on his shoulder, when he met a South African Police trooper – who, of course, attempted to arrest him. Mazweni threw down the meat and, as the trooper seized him to put on the handcuffs, he grabbed a fistful of sand which he threw in the policeman's eyes, getting away before the latter could remove it. Shortly after this Helfas arrested Mazweni again, and I asked the latter if the above story was correct. "Yes," he replied, "I wasn't going to be arrested, and I didn't want to hurt the white man, so I threw sand into his eyes!" After he had served his time for poaching in the Kruger National Park we handed him over to the Bushbuck Ridge Police, where he was tried for killing the sable.

Among a ranger's many duties he is supposed to have a little knowledge of first aid and medicine to enable him to doctor his native rangers and their families when they get sick – as medical  aid is usually far beyond their reach. Hardly a day passes but some woman or child or one of the men comes to be doctored. As a rule natives respond very well to treatment – even of the most amateurish kind: they are equipped with a goodly amount of faith and besides are very

hardy. But occasionally one strikes a very stubborn case, which no amount of the usually available medicine will cure.

I remember well a now-retired native ranger reporting sick and I diagnosed his condition as a malarial complication (a never-failing standby for all amateur doctors in the Lowveld). I treated him with the usual dosages of quinine, etc. but with no beneficial result and he gradually became worse. One day his son announced that he thought his father was going to die, and so, as I nourished a great regard for the old man and we had been hunting companions in the veld for many years, I saddled up my horse and rode over to his kraal. I entered his hut where he was lying and I at once realised that he was in a pretty bad way.

I must admit that I was really at a loss to know what to do for him, and then I remembered the remarkable faith natives have in anything novel in the way of cures. I went up to the sick man and said to him, "Can you hear me?" and he replied in a very weak voice, "Yes, Nkosi." I then said to him, "Tonight, when everyone else in the kraal is asleep, you must go out. If you cannot walk, you must crawl, but be careful that nobody sees you. When you get outside the door of your hut, turn to your right and then crawl or walk three times round the hut, and then sit down in the doorway and offer up a prayer to the spirits of your forefathers and then go back to bed and take these two tablets!" The tablets were, of course, quinine, though I had given him a lot before with no effect. I then told his son to come and report next day.

When the son appeared next morning I fully expected it was to announce the death of his father. Instead of this, however, he reported that my treatment had worked so well that the old man was very much better and was already looking around for something to eat! In a week's time he was quite fit again, though had it not been for the little superstitious suggestion I am sure he would not be alive today.

After some years of patrolling with pack donkeys I acquired a wagon and span of oxen and so could travel about in more comfort. Of course greater precautionary measures against lions were necessary and the oxen had to be tied to their yokes every night and large fires made. For this purpose I took more natives along with me, and during the day they would ride in the wagon so as to be fresh enough to cope with the firewood-collecting and scherm-making when we camped at sundown. The horses were always tied to the wheel of the wagon with riems made of waterbuck hide – which is very strong – and even if they did get frightened during the night they were unable to break the riems.

One night, when I was encamped on the Mbeamede spruit, two very big, black-maned lions attempted to enter the scherm, but the dogs gave the alarm and this, accompanied by the restlessness and snorting of the horses and oxen, awakened me. Crawling out from beneath the wagon where I was sleeping, I

fired a shot in the direction where the rustling of the grass indicated the lions' presence. They ran away and we were no more disturbed that night.

Early next morning, after a quick cup of coffee, I saddled my horse and took with me two of my best trackers and a couple of dogs. We soon picked up the spoor of the lions and it appeared that they had been hunting. After following their tracks for several miles we found where they had killed a wildebeest and eaten it, skin and all, leaving only the bones.

It was hard to believe that two lions could eat such a quantity of food in one night (in fact, within a few hours), but there could be no doubt about it as we had followed their spoor for miles and there were certainly only two of them. They must have been very hungry and quite empty when they had made their kill. At any rate, when they had finished dining they went down to a small pool nearby where they drank, as was evidenced from the fact that the water was still discoloured with the blood from the wildebeest that had evidently coated their faces and mouths.

From there they had travelled a short distance until, finding a nice shady tree in a patch of bare ground (whence they could see all round) they lay down to sleep off the effects of their huge meal. When we first saw them the lions were about one hundred and fifty yards away. I painstakingly crawled towards them in order to get a close shot, but I might have saved myself the pains! They had fallen into such a deep slumber – as a result of that gargantuan repast – that I could have walked right up to them without awakening them. The two lions were extended flat on their sides, so I whistled. The one heard me and raised his head and shoulder, and as I fired he just dropped back on his back with his four feet in the air – stone dead! I found later when skinning him that I had broken his neck.

The other lion, awakened by the shot, sprang up and trotted away, and as he ran I fired again and killed him too. These were two of the biggest lions I had shot so far. They were superb beasts with fine black manes, and I am very sorry now that I neglected then to take their measurements. Unfortunately in those days I worried little about such things.

CHAPTER 12
# UNWELCOME ENCOUNTERS

The possibility of finding snakes or scorpions among his bedding is a constant consideration with a game ranger using small, temporary camping places in the bush during his patrols. On more than one occasion, especially during the cool winter months, I have found a snake curled up in my blankets – no doubt attracted there by the warmth.

One evening, while patrolling up the Ngwanetsi River, we arrived at the waterhole just before sunset. While my native rangers were attending to the various jobs connected with making camp, such as collecting firewood and water, cutting thorny branches suitable for the surrounding scherm as a protection against lions and so forth, I took a sharp bush knife and cut some grass to form a warm and comfortable mattress on which to arrange my blankets. Every old bush camper knows, of course, that the only way to ensure a warm and comfortable night's rest in the bush, when sleeping on the ground, is to have plenty of cut grass beneath him. Without this the sleeper will almost certainly awaken stiff and shivering with cold during the night.

Having prepared my grass mattress and spread out my blankets, I ate my frugal supper, smoked a pipe or two and turned into bed early. It had been a hard, long day and I was very tired, so much so that although I heard a faint rustling in the grass beneath me during the night, I at first thought little of it. However, as the rustling grew louder and more pronounced, I decided that, nuisance as it was, it would be wise to investigate. Sitting up in bed I turned over the pillows and there, to my horror, lay a big *rinkhals* (black-necked cobra) curled up on the grass! Needless to say I jumped out of bed in double quick time, seized a piece of firewood and dispatched him.

Scorpions, also, are frequently a nuisance on these occasions as they sometimes creep into one's bed or one's clothes, and a scorpion's sting is extremely painful. One morning while pulling on my trousers I was badly stung on the leg by one of the little grey veld scorpions, and it was several seconds before I could kick the trousers off and kill it.

Of course, on most occasions when sleeping in the veld one doesn't undress, but goes to bed "all standing" (as the saying goes) in case one has to jump up in a hurry. The only articles of clothing generally removed are one's boots, and these are generally placed alongside the bed. One morning while pulling on my boots I was stung very badly by one of the big blue scorpions which are almost as large as small lobsters. The sting of these big scorpions is very poisonous, and although it very rarely causes death in a perfectly healthy human victim, should the latter be at all run-down by ill health it might well prove to be fatal.

I was in camp on the Imbabate River[15] one morning when one of my natives was brought to me. His face was in a terrible condition, his mouth being so swollen that he was unable to speak. When I asked him what was the matter he was unable to reply, but suddenly he had a brainwave and with his finger he drew in the sand a really excellent likeness of a scorpion (far better than anything I could have done), pointing to it and then to his mouth.

I therefore decided to remain over in that camp for the remainder of the day and by the next morning the swelling had subsided, and he was able to explain to me what had happened. It appeared that he was awakened from sleep by feeling something creeping across his head. Putting up his hand in the darkness to brush it off he must have annoyed a scorpion, which stung him in the lip before disappearing. In reply to my query as to how he knew it was a scorpion, he said that he could tell by feeling the shape.

During the course of one of my patrols we had occasion to cross a spruit near Ship Mountain in which were some big trees and rather thick bush. One of my native rangers, Bob, said to me, "Nkosi, this is where Mataffin was killed!" I asked him how he

---

[15] Timbavati River

knew and he told me that it was a long story, and he would tell it to me that night after we had got back to camp.

So that evening, while we sat before the merrily crackling campfire and an occasional soft gust of the night breeze scattered a shower of sparks among the softly curling fragrant woodsmoke, illuminating the silent, twisted, grotesque forms of the surrounding bush trees so that they seemed to have gathered around us in a watching, listening, ghostly audience, he related to me the story of how Mataffin was killed.

"You will remember, Nkosi, that Mataffin was a chief who came from Swaziland, with some of his followers, and settled where Mr H.L. Hall's farm is now. Madabula (Abel Erasmus), who was the Native Commissioner for these parts, told Mataffin that he and his people would have to pay taxes to the government, but this Mataffin refused to do. Madabula then sent some of his native police to arrest Mataffin, but they were beaten by his people and returned to report to Madabula.

"Mataffin now realised that he was in for trouble, and he thought that his best plan would be to leave the country. He could not return to Swaziland, so he decided that the best place for him would be Portuguese Territory. He sent on his wives by road to Crocodile Poort, which was then the terminus of the railway from Lourenço Marques, so that they could cross the border from there by train. Mataffin did not accompany his wives as he thought that the police were watching for him, but himself left on horseback, intending to strike the old Delagoa Bay road to Portuguese East Africa.

"He spent the first night at Nhliziyo's kraal, which was situated to the west of Ship Mountain. He was carrying with him, in his saddlebag, a bag of golden sovereigns, and unfortunately for Mataffin, Nhliziyo noticed this wealth. His discovery was all the more ill-omened for Mataffin in that Nhliziyo was a Basotho, having no love for the Swazis, who had frequently raided his people in the early days.

"Next day Nhliziyo offered to accompany Mataffin and guide him to a short cut which adjoined the Delagoa Road. Mataffin was unarmed, but Nhliziyo carried a rifle. He accompanied Mataffin as far as Ship Mountain and then intimated that he would leave him at this spruit, assuring him that he was almost on the road now and had just to keep to the path for a little further. As Mataffin rode away, Nhliziyo shot him in the back. He then shot the horse, took the bag of sovereigns and returned home to his kraal."

Bob went on to say that a few days later he happened to be hunting near that spot when he noticed a strong smell of "dead animal" and went to investigate. On entering the spruit he found the remains of the horse and also bits of Mataffin – bits the lions and hyenas had left – and the wax ring from his head, such as chiefs always used to wear woven into their hair. Bob lost no time in getting away from the evil spot, for at that time this was still a wild country; there was no law and order and no police, and so nothing was done to trace the murderer.

I knew Nhliziyo well and on several occasions during my patrols I had slept at his kraal. He was a Basotho, quite well off for a native, but he was always terribly mean. He would never buy himself a coat, seldom a blanket, and he was usually dressed in bits of game skin. He possessed quite a lot of cattle, the only herd not commandeered during the Boer War – his being the furthest kraal from the Boers' sphere of operations.

After the conclusion of the war he had a very nice herd, and as cattle were then very scarce he sold them to both white and black at high prices, and never spent the money. Owning a big kraal he had several wives and many grown-up sons who had married and lived near him. As years passed he grew old and ailing, and whenever he became sick he accused his sons and his wives of bewitching him and wanting to kill him so that they could get his money. He told them that they could have what was left of his cattle (he was killing and eating the latter as fast as he could), but that they should never have his money.

One day, when I was outspanned at his kraal, I could see that he was failing rapidly. I asked him what was going to happen to all his accumulated wealth, but he stubbornly replied that nobody was going to have that! Not long after this he died. Of course the family dug up the floor of his hut as, according to native custom, a man's wealth in money is always buried there, the excavation being carefully covered up again. Finding nothing, however, they energetically dug up the surrounding country, but still with no satisfactory results. They even brought witch doctors from the Portuguese Territory! But even these mighty and skilled men of mystery failed to divulge where this hardened old miser had deposited his ill-gotten wealth.

Nhliziyo's kraal was situated at the foot of a big, stony ridge covered with lots of loose boulders and slabs, and I feel sure that Mataffin's bag of sovereigns, and all the money Nhliziyo got for the sales of his cattle, lie buried beneath one of these rocks and there it will probably remain until doomsday. Should somebody, however, have the good fortune to discover it some day, it would be a good haul as it consisted entirely of gold sovereigns.

During the days before the advent of East Coast Fever and foot-and-mouth restrictions, when I could still trek about my section in my ox wagon, my wife frequently used to accompany me, and she also had her anxious moments!

I well remember one occasion when we were encamped at M'hlabantu, where I had a picket for my native rangers and a couple of huts for my own use. During the afternoon I had shot an old wildebeest bull for meat for ourselves and the men and we loaded this on the wagon and brought it into camp, where it was skinned and cut up into quarters. By the time the cutting up of the meat was finished it was too dark to do other than leave it on the wagon for the night, my intention being to hang the meat in a tree next morning.

During the night we were awakened by one of the men coming to report that there was a lion on the wagon, eating the meat. I had four big dogs with me, but they had been tied up inside the enclosure as lions had a pretty bad reputation at this camp, having recently killed two of my native rangers' dogs there. The dogs were barking furiously, but as they were tied up the lions took no notice of them – though the wagon was only about twenty yards from where they were tied. I hastily pulled on some more clothes (it was a cold winter's night), grabbed my rifle and went out, followed by my wife, who held the torch which she shone on the wagon.

I shall never forget the uncanny effect presented to us as the

glare of the torch fell on the wagon. The form of the lion was strongly illuminated against the dark background, its eyes glowing like burning coals as, its attention attracted in our direction, it stood glaring at us for a second before leaping from the wagon with a jolt that shook the whole vehicle, taking a shoulder of meat with it as it went. As it disappeared into the darkness I fired a shot after it.

My wife shone her torch all round, where we could hear rustling of grass in all directions, and reddish twin spots of fiery light appeared and as suddenly disappeared here and there like great moving stars, the eyes of several lions reflecting the torchlight. Now and then one caught glimpses of the palely illuminated, vague forms of the beasts as they slunk about among the herbage and trees. I think there must have been at least seven lions altogether, although only one of them had jumped on to the wagon. Meantime, all the dogs continued to bark furiously, adding greatly to the tense impressiveness of the scene.

At this moment one of the dogs, a big, heavily built one, managed to slip his collar and he came running excitedly to where my wife and I were standing. We were unable to hear his approach on account of the noise the others were making, and so you can imagine how my wife felt when, concentrating as she was on trying to focus her torch on the lions moving about in the bush around us, all of a sudden she felt a heavy body bump up against her legs! She said afterwards that her knees just seemed to give way beneath her, as she felt quite certain that it was a lion approaching from behind!

I fired a few more shots to scare off the lions, and after the dogs had quietened down we retired once more to spend the remainder of the night in peace.

Having told this yarn rather at my wife's expense, I feel I must follow it with another at my own.

At the end of a long, dry winter, the kudu, being pressed by hunger for at least something green to eat, began to jump the fence round our flower garden. I raised the fence by another couple of feet all round, which made it seven feet high, but even this

they seemed to clear quite easily. I then decided to tie up one of my dogs inside the fence in the hope that this would frighten the kudu away. During the night I heard the dog yelping most pitifully, as if something had caught him. I called out to my wife that the wretched lion had caught the dog and seizing my gun, rushed to the spot in the garden where he had been tied, my wife, as usual, following me with the torch.

Now, everybody is aware, I think, that roses are equipped bounteously with thorns, but I was made doubly aware of this fact that night. My wife, going ahead with the torch, could see the bushes and steer clear of them, but I followed in the darkness and, clad only in thin pyjamas and with bare ankles, seemed to bump into every rose bush with the longest and most vicious thorns, so that my pyjamas were torn and my legs badly scratched.

Eventually, accompanied by much profanity on my part, we ripped and tore our way to where the old dog (who was encouraging our approach with anxious whimpers) was tied up and there, right up against the outside of the fence and within a yard of the dog, were two lions. No wonder he was howling! As we appeared they trotted away and I sent a couple of No. 6 shots after them, which stung them up considerably, as they let out a couple of grunts.

I immediately loosened the poor old dog, feeling that he had certainly earned compassionate leave from further duty after that ordeal. Next morning, when I went to investigate, I found that the two lions had been scratching a big hole under the fence in their efforts to get at the dog. I raised the fence another foot, now making it eight feet high, and this successfully stopped the kudu from invading our garden.

One day while travelling by car I came upon four kudu cows standing alongside the road. Just as I came opposite them three of them bounded across just ahead of my car; the fourth remained standing in a very hesitant manner, so I thought that she was waiting for me to pass before joining her mates across the road. However, as I was in the act of passing her she evidently changed her mind for she leapt right over the bonnet of the car, successfully clearing it without the slightest touch!

Some time later one of the men engaged in drilling for water at the Pretorius Kop rest camp was returning from a trip to White River and had reached a point some two miles inside the Park from the gate. Suddenly a big kudu bull, hitherto invisible to the driver as it had been standing behind a clump of bush, jumped out and sprang right on to the car, shattering the windscreen and damaging the bonnet very badly. The kudu must have hit the car with its head, for it broke its neck and dropped dead beside the car. I am inclined to think that the driver was travelling a bit too fast, and this emphasises the necessity for a speed limit of twenty-five miles per hour when driving through the Park.

Most of the game animals killed in the Park by accidents with cars are victims of over-speeding. Numerous are the pretty little squirrels and smaller creatures killed in this way during the tourist season.

It is remarkable how a simple wire-netting fence, although only a few feet high, will keep a lion out. We have had such fences round the Kruger National Park rest camps for several years and lions have never yet been known to jump over them. On various occasions they have got through, but only when they have stampeded game feeding near the fence, right into it, so that it has been broken down by the blind, panicking rush of the animals. In one such instance the lions caught, killed and ate a kudu inside the rest camp at Pretorius Kop!

There seems to be no end to the queer things lions will do. While the water-boring operations were in progress I warned the man in charge not to leave any of his tools lying about during the night as lions would carry them off if they came around. However, he disregarded this advice, evidently thinking it was a typical piece of leg-pulling on my part. The result was, of course, that he lost his picks, shovels and also a bag of drilling shot.

It is a fact that lions will carry away anything they find bearing the human scent, and in most cases they will tear it or chew it to bits, such things as empty petrol tins being dented and punctured by the great canine teeth out of all hope of repair. One night a lion got his head in a bucket in which there remained some porridge left by the natives. As he did so the bucket handle slipped over his neck, which frightened him, and off he galloped with it into the veld. The bucket was found some distance away next morning, badly damaged.

While riding near Pretorius Kop I came upon a lion with a tin (it looked like a two-pound jam tin) stuck in his mouth. He was trying to clutch it out with his paw, but his big teeth must have punctured a hole in the metal and he seemed unable to remove it. As, needless to say, it was quite impossible for me to offer him any assistance, I just had to leave him, hoping that later on he would be able to scratch it off. As neither I nor my staff ever came across such a lion again in the course of subsequent patrols, I presume he must have freed himself of this embarrassing object!

In 1926, after the old Sabi and Shingwedzi game reserves had been converted into the present Kruger National Park, we were instructed not to shoot any more lions as they had proved a great attraction to visitors, and from then onwards there was no more lion hunting, except in circumstances where the beasts were giving trouble. So, instead of carrying a rifle wherever I went, I carried a fly whisk made out of a wildebeest's tail, as the game flies are very bad during the summer months and one has to keep the fly whisk moving all the time. These particular flies are very small, but they give a stinging bite.

One morning, as I was having my breakfast, the camp supervisor sent me a note saying that a tourist had reported having seen a jackal with a broken leg on the road. After breakfast I intended to investigate in my car, but found that my man had removed one of the tyres to mend a puncture, so I rode out on horseback instead. I saw a jackal, apparently a bit lame, hopping across the road, and it disappeared behind a bush about one hundred yards off the road.

Just before reaching the bush in question I heard a couple of grunts such as are usually uttered by an angry lion, and looking round I saw, on higher ground, a lioness galloping down straight towards me with a lion following closely on her heels. Pulling up my horse I shouted at her, at the same time vigorously waving my fly whisk. The lioness slackened her pace a little at this demonstration, but as she still came on in as determined a manner as ever I began to suspect that she might be after my horse.

It was an unheard-of thing for a lion to chase anyone on horseback in the Kruger National Park during the daytime – at least that was my experience – but I had forgotten that a few generations of lion cubs had been born and grown up since the days when we used to hunt lions as part of our routine and that they, as a result, probably did not fear so much of man as formerly.

I reflected that if I dismounted and revealed myself as a human being the lioness would probably stop, but by now she was pretty close and on second thoughts it occurred to me that if I allowed myself to be on the ground, unarmed, and the lioness still came on, the risk would be too great. I therefore dug my spurs into the pony and trusted to her speed. As I galloped through the long grass we ran almost on top of another lion that had been crouching there all the while. He flattened his ears and looked very cross, but fortunately did not pursue us and we managed to get away.

In this case I came to the conclusion that the reason why the lioness had chased me was because she had been mating with the lion who was following her, and I thought it very unlikely that such a thing would happen again, so I continued to ride about with only a fly whisk.

However, in this I was proved to be wrong!

Shortly afterwards I went out again, unarmed, on horseback, to inspect my gangs of labourers who were employed in road repairs, and as the horse I was riding was rather fresh, I decided to give him his head in a good long gallop down to the entrance gate and back. As we were galloping along I suddenly noticed two lionesses on my left, running straight for me – rather from the front than from the side. I pulled up and shouted loudly at them, at which they stopped and crouched in the grass, but presently came on slowly, crawling low on the ground. At first my horse did not notice them and seemed not unduly concerned, but he must have got a whiff of the wind as it took me all my time to make him face the lionesses.

While I was doing this the lionesses only approached slowly, but they increased their pace to a trot whenever the horse turned round. I kept on waving my switch at them, thinking this might scare them, but they still continued to advance, though slowly. I then took off my hat and waved it at them, but it made no difference – they still came on. I considered that if I did run for it, it would only mean one short rush on their part and the lions would be on us, as by now they were very close.

At this juncture the curb chain of the bit of my horse's bridle broke and with the chain off, pulling on the horse's mouth I had little control over him, so I desperately judged it best to let him go and make a bolt for it. In either case, it seemed, they might get me, and being a pretty fast horse that required no urging with lions after him, he galloped his hardest with one lioness grunting at his tail and the other ranging in the grass alongside of him! It was a nerve-wracking experience and I don't want any more of it, but, mercifully, we managed to outdistance our savage pursuers and safely got away.

As a result of this experience I ride about with a rifle once more, though only on one occasion have I been forced to use it. While riding through some short grass I noticed a lioness approaching my horse in a crouching attitude – very like that assumed by a cat when stalking a bird. I pulled up to see what she would do, but she still advanced. As I had my rifle with me this time I did not mind, so sat on my horse and watched her. I thought that my horse was the object of her attention and that the lioness was not aware of my presence and so I presently dismounted and walked about ten paces towards her.

To my astonishment, however, my action did not deter her in the least, for she continued to come on steadily, still in that half-crouching attitude. Suddenly I became aware of a second lioness, which had probably hitherto been hidden behind a little patch of bush, grimly advancing behind the other in the same silent, menacing way. They came closer and closer and then I realised that soon, with a short rush, they would have me. It seemed high time that they should be taught a lesson, so I shot the foremost lioness and the other bounded away into the bush.

Some time after this episode I sent my man with my horse to M'timba; he rode the animal for the eleven miles' distance and I followed in my car a little later. When I got to M'timba the man with the horse was waiting for me as usual. I asked him how he had got on and he replied that it had been very unpleasant as a lion had chased him and had very nearly caught the horse. It appeared that as he was riding along the path he heard a loud grunt from a patch of adjoining scrub and out rushed a lion.

My man lost no time in riding away as fast as he could with the lion in hot pursuit, and fortunately the horse was a quick one and it managed to outpace the lion. As he went galloping through the bush my man saw a herd of wildebeest in an open place and he rode straight for them, thinking that this might distract the lion. This sagacious manoeuvre on his part seemed to work, as the wildebeests scattered in all directions and the lion left him. He said that when he had ridden through a spruit some little distance away he glanced back and saw the lion standing in the open space where the wildebeests had been, looking in his direction.

This was, in fact, the second time this particular man had been chased by lions. Previously to this, at the end of a very rainy season, I went to inspect the Jock of the Bushveld road. As the road had been very badly washed in places I was unable to travel far along it by car and so I sent this same native on ahead on an old horse of mine called Dobbin, to await me at a certain spot where I could leave the car and take the horse.

I rode along the road for about ten miles, noticing where it was badly washed out and needed repair, and when I returned to the car it was already sundown. I handed the horse over to the man, telling him not to loiter on the road during the four miles home as it would soon be dark and there were lions about. I then gave him about half an hour's start and followed slowly in the car.

As I did not catch up with him soon I began to wonder what had happened, and presently I got out of the car to see whether I could find his spoor as it was still just light enough to see. Sure enough, there was the horse's spoor – but the ground was dug up by it and it was clear that the horse had been galloping, and superimposed over it was the spoor of lions. It. was quite clear, in fact, that he had been chased by them. The only thing to do was to proceed, and before going much further I saw four young lions in the road, looking excited and twitching and waving their black-tipped tails restlessly. Passing them, I soon after heard the drumming of the horse's hooves on the road ahead and when I got near enough, I saw the man and horse still going hell for leather.

Yelling at him to stop, I got out of the car and found poor old Dobbin coated in white lather from head to foot. I was angry with the man for galloping my poor old horse so hard and spoke strongly to him, but he explained that, after leaving me, he had

come on four young lions which had chased him hard and nearly caught him. I suggested that perhaps they were only playing with him, but he vigorously denied this, saying, "When one lion runs behind you and the others gallop alongside, they don't mean play!"

I then accompanied the man, travelling very slowly in the car, until we reached home. Next morning poor old Dobbin was so stiff that he could hardly walk. He was then a long way behind his prime and he had proved to be a faithful servant to me. Had the man not been a good rider, both he and the horse would surely have been caught that time.

Two years after this I sadly assisted old Dobbin into the Happy Grazing Grounds with a merciful .303 bullet.

CHAPTER 13

# SNAKES

The hot, dry Lowveld of the Eastern Transvaal is one of the most snake-infested regions in Africa, though during the cool winter months, when most people visit the Kruger National Park, snakes are less in evidence and less active than in summer. Most people dislike and fear these reptiles, on the other hand tales true (and even untrue!) about them are usually popular; and so, since in the course of my long years of service in what is now the Kruger National Park I have had my share of interesting experiences with these reptiles, I will devote this chapter to a few of the more remarkable incidents.

At M'timba one day I was leaning over the edge of the table in order to pick up something when suddenly it seemed as if two red-hot needles had pierced my eyes. Instinctively and with horror I realised that, although I had not seen the snake, my eyes had received a dose of venom from a spitting cobra, locally known as a rinkhals (actually the true rinkhals, *Sepedon haemachates*[16], does not

---

[16] *Hemachatus haemachatus*

occur in the Eastern Transvaal Lowveld and this was a black-necked spitting cobra, Naja nigricollis — a brownish-grey snake, yellow-white below with a dark band across the throat). This snake has the power of ejecting its venom in the form of a fine spray for a distance of a few feet, and it is remarkably accurate in aiming at the eyes of its assailant.

There was a dish of water standing in the room, so I groped my way towards it and washed my eyes out well with soap and water. In the meantime I called my men to come and kill the snake.

I had heard that fresh milk was an effective first-aid antidote so I continued to bathe my eyes with it for a couple of days. In addition to the fresh milk, I washed them in a solution of permanganate of potash.

My eyes were very painful and I was quite blind for three days and had to remain in a dark room, but gradually, to my unbounded relief, my eyes recovered completely. I think that if one of these spitting cobras was to spit into one's eyes out in the veld, when a long way from water or any other aid, one would probably be permanently blinded.

One of the native attendants in the rest camp at Pretorius Kop went out one afternoon to collect firewood. As he stooped down to collect some dry branches a black-necked cobra spat venom into both his eyes, causing total blindness. Being, of course, unable to locate the correct direction of the camp, he shouted for aid, but apparently nobody heard him. So he wandered desperately about, searching vainly for the camp, until darkness fell. He then wisely decided that the best thing to do would be to stay where he was, in the hope that a search party might be sent out for him. However, since nobody had noticed him leave the camp, it was thought that he had merely visited his kraal.

This unfortunate native said that during the night he heard lions grunting at no great distance from where he crouched, but fortunately for him they had made a kill. At dawn the next morning he heard the cocks crowing in the compound and realised with relief that he was not far from the camp; so he renewed his shouts and presently he was heard and the men came out and found him and brought him back to me. He was still quite blind and his eyes were badly inflamed. I washed his eyes out with permanganate and repeated the treatment several times, which was quite successful as he regained his sight after a few days. However, it was two or three weeks before his eyes were quite normal again; no doubt because they were not attended to at once.

I have lost a number of dogs through snakes, especially mambas, and on one occasion I lost seven dogs at once, all killed by one mamba! In this instance my dogs had put up the snake from a patch of grass, run him down, and now stood round him barking. One dog would rush in, and the snake would strike with such speed that we could hardly follow its action. The dog would let out a yelp and in a few minutes it would be dead. Unfortunately it was quite impossible for me to interfere as the thor-

oughly excited dogs were all mixed up with the snake, and had I fired at the latter I would almost certainly have killed some of the dogs as well.

The remaining dogs, after the fourth or fifth dog had succumbed, took longer to die – I expect on account of the gradual lessening of the quantity of venom with each additional bite. I could do nothing as I had no serum with me at the time, and all of the dogs finally died. I revenged them all, however, by shooting the snake at the first opportunity.

One day when going for a walk about two miles from my house I saw two mambas, in a patch of scrub, wrapped round each other. This was such an astonishing spectacle that I watched them for quite a while. About four or five feet of their lengths were raised above the ground – presenting a remarkable and rather horrifying sight – and I think they must have been mating as they were sufficiently absorbed in one another to take no notice of myself, though I stood watching them not far away.

Having no firearms with me, not even a stick, I finally returned home for a shotgun – rather doubting whether I would find them again on my return. However they were still there, behaving exactly as when I left them, twining and untwining themselves about each other. This time I shot them both, but unfortunately was unable to distinguish between the sexes.

Quite recently when talking to an old native named Charlie about the above incident he told me that a new kraal had been built close to the spot concerned. A party of natives on their way to a beer-drink had occasion to pass the almost identical patch of scrub, and there, to their astonishment, they witnessed a similar spectacle.

Finally about fifteen natives had gathered and they were standing round the two snakes talking and shouting as only natives can, and yet the two mambas took not the slightest notice of them, being, as previously, completely concerned with each other. One of the natives returned to Charlie's kraal and obtained a long stick with which they finally killed the snakes while they were still entwined.

The black mamba is, I suppose, the best known (as it is certainly the most feared) of African snakes, so perhaps I may recount another experience or two about this very deadly reptile.

I happened one day to be riding through some short grass when I saw a mamba travelling towards my horse. He was coming on at a good pace and was already, when I first noticed him, so close that I thought my safest plan was to pull up and stand still. Fortunately the horse failed to see the snake, and being unaware of its presence was not frightened and remained quite still.

The mamba passed right under its belly and entered an old, disused ant heap a few yards beyond. I wasted no time in placing a good distance between us! In this case the snake clearly had no aggressive intentions: it simply wanted to enter its hole in the ant heap, but had it been suddenly alarmed at such close quarters and fancied its retreat cut off it would almost certainly have struck with fatal results – at any rate to the horse.

Two native women were visiting at the kraal of one of my native rangers. They had only just arrived and were sitting down and gossiping with the other women, while one was holding up her small baby, when suddenly a whirlwind came along, pursuing its tortuous, violent course straight towards where the women were sitting. Two of them sprang up and ran away to escape the accompanying dust, but the woman with the baby could not get away so quickly. Suddenly a mamba appeared, apparently from among the dust, and made straight for the woman with the baby. Raising its forepart off the ground, as a mamba will, the snake struck savagely at the woman, who, screaming with terror, clutched the baby to her breast. Curiously enough, it missed the baby but struck the mother in the chest and then passed on.

The other women, hearing her cries, returned and asked whether she had been bitten by the snake. She replied that she was not sure, but that there was a burning sensation in her chest. As nothing could be done she very shortly died. Of course the general opinion was that the snake had been deliberately sent by someone to kill her.

Shortly after this incident had taken place, I was passing by the same kraal with my lorry when I saw a mamba stretched across the road, basking in the sun. The lorry passed over it, injuring its back, so that it could only crawl very slowly, and I got off and shot it. On measuring it I found it to be twelve feet long. After that no more mambas were seen at that kraal, so probably this was the snake that had killed the woman.

On another occasion, while living at M'timba, I was walking at the back of the camp, just beyond the fence, when I saw a very big black mamba retreating into a patch of scrub. As I had no gun with me I left him there and went on. Some time later, while passing the place on my way back, I saw my small son standing in the middle of that patch of scrub with his air gun, evidently looking for *toppies* that were eating our fruit. I felt a cold shiver run down my spine, knowing how deadly mambas were, and not wishing to alarm him and cause a commotion I quietly said, "Henry! Come here!" Fortunately the snake made no appearance, so I told him there was a mamba in the scrub and not to go back there again.

One day I was walking below my vegetable garden in a small donga when I heard the rustling of dead leaves. Glancing in that direction I beheld a mamba coming towards me. I did not like to turn and run as I thought that by doing so I might tempt him to chase me, so I quietly backed away as fast as I could – which was not nearly quick enough for my liking! I kept my eyes on him all the time, noticing with satisfaction that his pace was gradually slowing down, and finally he stopped. I then turned and ran as fast as I could to the house, collected my shotgun and returned, but the snake had gone.

Next to mambas, pythons rank as the most sensational of African snakes, and there are plenty of them in suitable places in the game reserve. Dogs sometimes have narrow escapes from these huge snakes, and sometimes they are not so lucky.

One day I was out riding with my pack of dogs when I heard them barking ahead as if they had something baled up in the bush. I galloped in the direction indicated, but my arrival was slightly delayed by a patch of thickish bush through which I had to pass. Having, however, finally come up with the barking mob, I dismounted and entered the patch of scrub in which the clamour was taking place and found that they had surrounded a python – an exceptionally large one too!

A well-placed bullet dispatched the snake, and on looking round to see that all my dogs were there, I discovered that one dog – a fox terrier – was missing. I then noticed a suspiciously big bulge in the python's stomach, and thinking that this might account grimly for the terrier's absence I quickly ripped open the snake with my sheath knife. There, sure enough, was my fox terrier. At first I thought he was dead, but after a short while there seemed to be a movement in his legs and gradually he recovered and stood up – apparently none the worse for having been swallowed by a python!

That lions apparently sometimes attack and eat pythons was suggested to me by the following interesting experience.

I was travelling in my car along the Jock of the Bushveld road one day when I noticed a lion standing a few yards away from the road, intently gazing at something on the ground. Upon stopping the car, in order the better to see what was interesting the lion, I observed that it was a large python with half its body coiled. The lion stepped up close to the snake, whereupon the latter immediately struck at him, but the lion dodged the blow. The next time the python lunged the lion jumped forward and, grabbing the snake in his jaws, almost bit it in two. He then proceeded to eat a bit of the snake,

finally lying down beside it. Having seen enough I then drove on. When I returned later in the day I halted at the spot but neither python nor lion was there: most likely the lion had in due course eaten up the remainder of the snake.

While on patrol with two of my native rangers near Ship Mountain we found a python basking in the sun, asleep. As at the time I wanted the skin, I shot him – the bullet entering just at the back of his head and appearing to be fatal. I ordered my native rangers to take off the skin but they answered that they were afraid to do so and disliked touching a snake, even if it was dead! They informed me, however, that native ranger Sokis, whom we had left behind in camp, did not share their prejudice in this respect. So we left the python there and returned with Sokis next morning.

Sons took out his sheath knife and caught hold of the python by the tail in order to straighten it (as it was all curled up) before skinning. Now, the python had hitherto appeared to be perfectly dead and, in fact, had remained here all night; but no sooner had Sokis clutched its tail than it became very much alive, and made off (with Sokis still hanging on) towards an old antbear hole, about fifteen yards away, in which it evidently lived.

It was rapidly disappearing down the hole when one of the other native rangers, his excitement overcoming his fear, went to Sokis' assistance. Pull as they would they were quite unable to prevent the huge snake from finally escaping and since we had nothing with which to dig him out, and were some distance from camp, we had to leave that old python winner of the day!

To end this chapter on a superstitious note: I have often heard old natives talk about a wonderful snake known as muhlambela. Nobody has ever actually seen this serpent, but they all know someone who has seen it, or who knows somebody else who has seen it. It is said to be a big snake about twelve feet long that grows feathers on the back of its head and can bleat like a buck, which it does to attract people. It then strikes them on the back of the head with its fangs, never the front of the head. I regard this personally as pure superstition – flavoured strongly perhaps, with the mendacious propaganda and possible former practices of witch doctors – but herewith offer it for what it may be worth.

In this connection I would like to quote from an article written by my friend Mr Astley-Maberley:

The snake known as Muhlambela, as described by Mr Wolhuter, is of great interest because its existence, appearance, and habits are claimed by various tribes, with small local variations, almost throughout Tropical Africa! For instance, in the foothills and mountainous country to the west of the Kruger National Park, in the Duivelskloof and Tzaneen areas, this fabulous snake is called Noga A Thaba by BA-LOBEDU: and it is described as being hundreds of feet long clad in vivid, rainbow-like colours, and decorated with three feathers on the top of its head! Its habits are similar to those described by the Low-Veld natives: i.e., it attracts people by uttering a croaking or bleating call, and then "pecks" a neat hole in the back of their heads; killing them instantly (whence the reason that no living person claims to have seen it). Further, this snake is said to travel along the tops of the trees, and to inhabit the deepest and most forested kloofs. Its head is said to resemble that of a chameleon!

Certain deep kloofs in the mountains are shunned by natives on account of their being said to be inhabited by such snakes.

I have on several occasions investigated the raucous bleating and chattering cries attributed to this mysterious monster by Natives (much to their alarm!), and in all cases hitherto the sounds have been satisfactorily identified as rightly proceeding from the larger of our two local Lemurs (commonly known as "Bush-babies" or "Nagapies"), the Great, or Thick-tailed Galago

(*Otolemur crassicaudatus*). This creature only calls at night; and among a superstitious people fear and ignorance concerning its call could long be retained.

The probable explanation is that, possibly originally such places might have been inhabited by exceptionally old and aggressive mambas, and that, later, witchdoctors, in the interests of their nefarious pursuits, wishing to frighten people from entering secluded places wherein they kept special medicines, etc., invented the legendary monsters, using the mysterious nocturnal cries to lend colour to their assertions. This would also explain the fact that misguided intruders were undoubtedly found dead in former times, with "neat round holes always in the backs of their heads!"

At any rate, in parts of Nyasaland, East and Central and West Africa, wherever Bantu tribes live in bushy or forested country, beliefs concerning a snake with all the above attributes (with very small local variations in detail) occur, which proves that they must be of ancient origin. It is interesting to collect all possible information on this subject while there is yet time.

## Chapter 14

# RAINMAKERS

During one of my early patrols in the old Sabi Game Reserve I was riding along the bank of the Sabi River when I suddenly came upon the ruins of a brick-built house. The ruins of this house may still be seen; they are not far from where Number One Hippo Pool is now located, about fifteen miles from Pretorius Kop.

As I first saw them it was obvious that these ruins represented remains of a well-built three-roomed house and no doubt it had been originally roofed with thatch. Mr C.A. Yates, who was accompanying me at the time, took a photograph of this surprising discovery in the midst of the trackless, uninhabited bush (as it then was), and it can be seen, from this photograph, that big wild fig trees had grown up inside what was formerly the interior of the house. This is a significant fact, because these wild figs are usually very slow growing and I would estimate therefore that the ruins must have been nearly one hundred years old when we found them.

We were both exceedingly interested in our discovery and I made enquiries from the oldest natives living near the place, who informed me that "Jowawa", a Portuguese trader and hunter, had built the house and had lived there. Now this "Jowawa" (as he is known to the native peoples of the Lowveld) was a most remarkable and romantic character. His full name was Joao Albasini and Colonel J. Stevenson-Hamilton has written what is known about him in his *The Low-Veld: Its Wild Life and Its People*. Albasini was probably the first European to set foot in, or at least to settle in (certainly the only one to have left any legend or record) the Eastern Transvaal Lowveld.

My old native informants told me that "Jowawa" (who had certainly made a great impression among the contemporary local tribesmen and had become almost a legendary figure among their descendants) used to send his native hunters to the north (which I suppose is now the country between the Olifants and the Pafuri) to shoot elephants and bring him back the ivory, which he then sent to Delagoa Bay by carriers. He also traded ivory and buffalo, giraffe and hippo hides from the natives living round about his residence on the Sabi. Game, of course, abounded in those days, and elephants and most likely rhinoceros were a good deal more plentiful than they are today.

The natives informed me that "Jowawa" became chief over a large following, whom he assisted and protected against the Swazi raiders; and he was evidently a type who might easily have walked out of the colourful and adventurous pages of some of the late Sir Rider  Haggard's African romances! He must have been quite an enterprising man as he took out a water furrow about two miles in length from the Sabi and irrigated some very rich soil near his house, planting orchards and corn.

Later on I found an old native woman named Leya – who was then living with her people of the Mambayi tribe below the Berg near Spitzkop – who told me that, at that time, she lived with her family near Ship Mountain in the Lowveld when they were raided by the Swazis, who killed all the men and took the women and children back to Swaziland with them as their slaves. A few years afterwards she was sold to "Jowawa" as a slave, but she had no idea of the amount paid for her. She grew up in Albasini's household as a nursemaid to his children. She said that he married a Dutch girl, but she was unable to tell me from where his wife came.

After working for Albasini for some years she was given in marriage to one of his indunas, but she never had any children and when her husband died she was liberated. Hearing that some of her relatives had since settled below the Berg near Spitzkop she ultimately made her way there, and here she remained until her death many years later.

I remember this old native woman well as she was exceptionally fat, and

whenever she laughed (which, as in the case of most fat persons, was often) her whole body used to quiver and shake like the proverbial blancmange.

When "Jowawa" Albasini finally left Mgomenye[17] (which was the name of his home on the Sabi) he trekked to, and settled in, the Spelonken in the Zoutpansberg district of the Northern Transvaal, and most of his considerable body of followers accompanied him. Few white men have led a more remarkable existence in Africa, and a full account of his life and history, should it ever become available for publication, would be of great interest.

Anybody who has lived many years among the natives of Africa cannot fail to have had brought home to him the dominant role played by superstition in their lives. For centuries past the African mind has been so influenced by superstitious custom, fear of evil spirits, ghosts, witchcraft and so on, that not only the rural natives, but also all the semi-educated, as well as a goodly proportion of the genuinely more sophisticated natives, still remain willing victims of these ancient beliefs; though most of them would dislike to admit it.

However, many of these superstitions are very interesting in themselves and in the course of my life among the still fairly primitive native inhabitants of the Transvaal Lowveld I have been able to glean a few facts that are worth setting down here.

First let us deal with the rainmaker: since rain being most

---

[17] Manungu

essential for the growth of crops, water for cattle, etc., the individual who claims to have the means of controlling its incidence is of the utmost importance to the community. In the district of which I write rain was held to be brought by the native rainmaker Mpunzane Mhowelela. He was a M'Sotho (Basotho); and while still a boy he left his kraal, which was at the foothills of the Berg below Spitzkop,  and went to work for the white man – eventually getting as far as Port Elizabeth, which in those days was a long way from home.

After many years' wandering, Mpunzane returned to his kraal. He was then a grown-up man and he took to himself two wives. His old mother was still alive and, as she belonged to a "rainmaking" family, she imparted the jealously guarded secret knowledge of the craft to her son. This can only be done from the maternal side, as the child to whom this gift is passed must drink from the inspired breast, and although the father may be a rainmaker, his children will not inherit the ability from him.

The rainmaker has a small hut hidden in the dense bush of a kloof or a deep spruit where he conceals all his rainmaking medicines, and should anybody accidentally happen upon the place they will immediately turn back and run for their lives! They will know that it is a rainmaker's hut as soon as they come near it because a great feeling of instinctive fear will assuredly assail them so that their hair stand on end with fright. And, indeed, there is good reason for this, for many dreadful things are said to be included among the various ingredients of the rainmaker's unsavoury brew.

On occasions of every severe drought a rainmaker is sometimes compelled to offer up a human sacrifice to the rain spirit;

 but his sacrifice must always be one of his own blood, either one of his own children, grandchildren or some other member of his family. I am told that some of the deaths reported to me from Mpunzane's family when his kraal was still in the old game reserve (an area since excised and now in the adjoining native reserve) were not natural deaths, but in reality deliberate murders as sacrifices to the rain god.

Although the natives may have a very shrewd idea as to the truth, they will never talk about it; so it can be seen that a rain-maker's job is a sinister one. Usually a collection of money is made from all the natives living in that district at the commencement of the planting season, and when the time has come for the crop to be planted or sown, this is taken by one of the headmen and presented to the rainmaker. The latter then tells them that all will be well and that they must now go home and prepare to plant the crop. If the spirits are in good mood the requisite rain comes and the crops are planted and start to grow. Perhaps, after a few weeks or a month, another rain is required as the crops are, perchance, showing signs of drought, and then another collection is made.

Should the rains not come in time, however, the rainmaker always has a good excuse handy, such as, for instance, that some of the natives have not contributed to the fund or that the latter was not sufficient, or that some of them had started to plant the seed before permission had been granted by him with the result that, though sufficient money had been collected, the spirits had been angered. The addition of some more money would, in the latter case, probably propitiate the (somewhat materially minded!) spirits.

I remember, during one very dry season, some of the headmen of the local kraals, principally Mambayi, coming to me with the request that I would send for Mpunzane and tell him that he must make rain and that it was just pure "cussedness" on his part that he had hitherto continually refrained from doing so. To my question as to why they did not do this themselves they replied that they themselves were afraid of taking so direct a line in case Mpunzane was so angered that it would never rain again.

They finally decided among themselves – since I had refused to interfere in their customs – that discretion was the better part of valour and that it might be more politic to try a little soft-soaping, so they presented the obdurate Mpunzane with two head of cattle. The happy result of this was that down came the rain shortly afterwards.

On another occasion, during a long, dry summer, the usual collection was made, but with no resulting rain. While riding to Sabi Bridge (now Skukuza) one day I noticed that heavy rain had fallen at Doispane's. This was just one of the local showers which very often occur in these parts and the area affected only covered about one mile in extent. Anyhow, it fell on Doispane's land and his crops were saved, but no rain had fallen on other native lands more to the west and the thickly populated parts. On my return to M'timba I mentioned this to one of my policemen, saying, "Why cannot Mpunzane send the rain on his own crops? He cannot be a very good rainmaker!" He replied, "Nkosi, don't you know that Doispane took £1 to give to Mpunzane, and that is why rain fell on

Doispane's land! Mpunzane cares not whether rain falls on his own land or not as he has plenty of money with which to buy food, and so he does not depend for food on what he can grow!"

Once a year a party from the king's kraal in Swaziland visited Mpunzane to ask for rain. They had to report at my camp on their way, but they would never disclose the nature of their errand although I naturally had a pretty shrewd idea. They usually sojourned at Mpunzane's for a few days before returning to the royal kraal; and on one occasion Mpunzane told them not to be too long on returning home as rain was imminent. However, they must have travelled too slowly as the day after they had left a very heavy rain fell and they nearly got washed away in some of the spruits they had to traverse en route to the Crocodile River – which, of course, they had also to cross in due course. As it was, they found the river in flood and they had to wait several days on its bank before the water had subsided sufficiently.

I had on several occasions spoken to Mpunzane about his rainmaking. He was a very astute old man and his reply inevitably was, "Nkosi, no human being can make rain, only God!" I asked him why he accepted the natives' money and the cattle which they brought him to induce him to make rain, and he readily admitted that they offered him and that he accepted these things, but really, of course, merely because he was their chief!

Most noted rainmakers have a big following and eventually they become self-appointed chiefs on account of their fabulous gift.

When compulsory cattle dipping came into force against East Coast Fever, the government built several dipping tanks in the old game reserve and each ranger was made responsible for the dipping of cattle in his section and the maintenance of the dips to the requisite strength. I well remember the first day the cattle were put through the dip known as the Sand River dipping tank, where Mpunzane and his people lived. There were about eight hundred head of cattle and it was no easy matter inducing them to jump into the tank for the first time. Each struggling beast had to be pushed, carried and levered with long poles to get him in, and of course all the owners of the cattle and Mpunzane himself were there. It was a terribly hot summer's day and it was late in the afternoon before we had finished.

I then got busy giving each cattle owner his "chit" as to how many cattle he had as the same number had to be present for dipping every week, so a list of all these was entered in my book. When I was about halfway through this job, sitting under a tree with the natives in a circle all round me and old Mpunzane sitting beside me, the sky became a bit overcast but I did not expect rain just then. Suddenly, however, one of those short, sharp little showers – so frequent at that time of the year – descended upon us abruptly.

Looking up from my writing I turned to Mpunzane and asked him what he was doing. His usual cunning old smile spread gradually across his countenance and then a most curious thing happened, for Mpunzane looked up at the sky and, almost immediately it seemed, the rain stopped! From behind me I heard an old native whisper rather loudly that this was further proof of Mpunzane's greatness as a rainmaker in that he could make or stop rain at will. The old man's prestige was greatly enhanced by this incident.

Mpunzane died at his kraal about twelve years ago. His son Mdingane then took over in his father's stead as his mother was also from a rainmaking family, but although he carried on with varying success for a few years there was a lot of rivalry between his younger brother and himself, with the result that Mdingane was "bewitched" and died while receiving "medical" attention on the north bank of the Sabi, which was outside his rainmaking district, and he was buried there and not at his own kraal.

His son, who could maintain the family tradition, is sufficiently wise in his own generation to have nothing to do with his mystic birthright. He says that he values his life too much and that if he set up rainmaking he is fearful of being bewitched by his sinister uncle, who continues to practise in a half-hearted way, but with no great following either as a chief or as a rainmaker, being a drunken, useless character respected by none.

Another noted rainmaker was Matibela (also of the Mhowelela family). His sphere of operations extended from the north bank of the Sabi to the foothills of the Berg and up to the Olifants River. He died about ten years ago. He also practised with varying success and, being a rainmaker, was a self-appointed chief.

Occasionally during a very dry season he would come and ask my permission to go and *pahla* (i.e., speak to the spirits of his ancestors) at a sacred place at the foot of a small kopje called Kivenene, about eight miles south of Pretorius Kop. I always granted him permission and sent two of my native rangers to accompany him, each leading a goat that was killed and skinned and the meat placed on the ancestral grave while Matibela *pahla*'d to the spirits. None of the meat was eaten as it had to be left on the grave, but I suspect that pretty soon after the party had left the hyenas and other wild animals attended to that!

Sometimes this journey proved climatically fruitful, but in the event of adverse results Matibela could always find an acceptable excuse. I hear that his son has now taken his place – with fairly promising portents, as recently a very heavy rain fell north of the Sabi, which was accredited to him!

A firmly-rooted native belief is that nobody dies a natural death. When anybody dies, or becomes ill, he or she has been bewitched by some malevolently disposed individual; and in the case of a death, if the family is sufficiently interested in the individual concerned, the first step taken by the bereaved relatives is a visit to the local witch doctor. This highly respected individual claims to divine, either by throwing the bones (*dolossè*) or by going into a trance, who the culprit is, with the result that a certain party is indicated as being the guilty one.

The bereaved family then proceeds to the person who has thus been "smelt out" by the witch doctor and accuses him (or her) of having cast an evil spell over the deceased, thereby achieving the latter's death. The accused naturally denies this and finally he demands that they shall all consult the big witch doctor who lives across the border in Portuguese East Africa.

First of all they consult the chief, to whom they report the dispute, and he declares that it is advisable that the case be taken to the big witch doctor (mungoma). Each side agrees to pay so many head of cattle should the verdict be unfavourable to them. Then both parties retire home to prepare food for the journey, which takes about a fortnight there and back. A suitable day, previously agreed upon by both parties, is appointed for the commencement of the journey.

Each party usually comprises four to six individuals and as they had to come to me for a permit enabling them to travel through the game reserve to Portuguese territory, I was acquainted with the reason for such consultations and also learnt the results on their return. Usually there are two or more women in attendance to carry the food for their menfolk. When they reach Portuguese territory, enquiries are made as to which is the best witch doctor, as several noted diviners practise there.

Shortly before they arrive at the selected doctor's residence the principal parties on both sides hide some money – usually two shillings or two shillings and sixpence – on their persons; perhaps it is concealed in their hats, or a boot, or on any other portion of the body. This is to test the power of the witch doctor: if he is any good he will straight away remove the money from where it is hidden.

Usually they find a big crowd of people assembled at the mungoma's kraal – all there for the same purpose as themselves – and they have to await their turn. When this is indicated, all enter the presence of the mungoma in a body, well mixed up, this being an additional test for the mungoma, who has to sort them out into their correct parties. He then informs them of his fee (which is anything from three to five pounds) and this is handed over to him. The serious business of "smelling out" the guilty person then begins.

Having separated the two groups concerned, the *mungoma* produces a specially prepared drink in a small earthenware pot of which both the complainant and the accused have to imbibe. I expect that he has already made up his mind which of the two individuals is to be the guilty one, so when handing the drink to that particular party he perhaps introduces cleverly into the liquid a little quantity of a very strong nerve poison of some sort known to the witch doctors and probably concealed under his thumbnail for the purpose.

At any rate, after about half an hour the poison takes effect and one of the two who have each drunk from the same pot begins to behave in a most queer manner, going through the strangest antics; barking like a dog or a baboon or howling like a hyena; sometimes even imitating the roar of a lion. He has, in fact, become "drunk with *mpondo*" and presently he performs the gruesome actions of pretending to cut and eat bits of flesh from his imaginary victim, and this, of course, is unanimously accepted as proof positive that he is, in very truth, the culprit.

When, after recovering from the effects of the *mpondo*, the bewildered and terrified wretch is sufficiently confused to admit his own guilt, the triumphant witch doctor then puts a nick in his ear to certify his guilt. Both parties accept the verdict without hesitation and having packed up their belongings they return to their kraals, and the chief finally settles the matter (which, in olden times, would probably have meant a tortured death for the condemned).

This, of course, is contrary to European law, but it is going on all the time and nothing will finally stop it for a very long time.

The ordinary witch doctor also inherits this gift from his mother's side, as it must come through her milk. There are female as well as male witch doctors, and should one native harbour a grudge against another, the former goes to a witch doctor and pays him so much to kill his enemy by witchcraft, or to cast a spell over him which will cause him to become very sick and die a lingering death.

So powerful is the effect of suggestion upon the superstitious African native that, should he have reason to believe that such a spell has been cast upon him he is quite likely to sicken and even ultimately die, through sheer fear – even though he may be perfectly fit before such an idea enters his head.

Witches (ba-loyi) also have the power of converting themselves into wild animals, the better to pursue their evil deeds. The favourite animal chosen is the hyena, and sometimes also a lion, as both these animals travel about by night when all decent people are asleep.

Some witches also have the power to send lightning to kill people, and a native will never as a rule build a new kraal without first calling a "lightning doctor" to protect his kraal against lightning. The doctor hammers in four hardwood pegs round the kraal and on these he rubs some medicine to keep the lightning away, but should the unfortunate owner of the kraal have his hut struck by lightning later on the doctor always has a suitable excuse, such as, "You should have come to me with a second payment to renew the medicine on the pegs!" – and so on.

A native will never pass under a tree that has been struck by lightning, nor will he use its wood for firewood, as something evil would be sure to happen to him were he to do so.

Like quite a number of Europeans, natives believe that should an owl perch on the roof of a hut and hoot several times, it is a sign that somebody who lives in that hut will die before long.

Another quaint native superstition is that of pulling the finger and toe joints of a person injured in an accident or in a fight. If the finger and toe joints are pulled by the person responsible for the accident the patient will make a speedy recovery. If these precautions are not taken, it is believed that the victim may die.

A rather dramatic instance of the strength of this belief was brought home to me by the case of one of my own men. While at a beer-drink he was hit on the head with a knobkerrie, causing a very nasty wound. His opponent refused to pull his finger joints when requested to, so he collected his rifle and returned to the kraal in question. He then asked his opponent once more to pull his finger joints, but on this being refused he shot him dead. Of course, he was still under the influence of beer at the time.

After shooting his stubborn adversary, my man returned to my camp and gave himself up to my native corporal, who in turn arrested him. It happened that I was away on leave at the time, so my corporal-in-charge handed the man over to the police and in due course, after my return from leave, all this was reported to me.

I then went to the gaol at Nelspruit and located my native; and as he had hitherto always been a good fellow, I interested myself in his case. During an interview with him he told me all that had occurred and why he had shot the other fellow, adding sombrely that all that was left now was for the white man to hang him, and that he was quite willing to give his own life in return for the life he had taken.

I asked him whether he would like me to engage defence for him when his case came before the court, but he reiterated his willingness to die and would not hear of being defended. Later on, when the case came up at Circuit Court, I again had a long talk with him – thinking that, after being confined in gaol for some months, he might have changed his mind, but he remained as obdurate as before, repeating his original affirmation that the white man's law was a "life for a life", and that he was willing to forfeit his.

However, the next time I visited the prisoner I took with me an advocate and this appeared to impress him, for he finally agreed to be defended legally. After listening to the case the advocate said that the circumstances did not warrant his being able to put up much of a defence, until I mentioned the custom of pulling the fingers, and he then agreed that, though not very promising, the whole defence rested on that point.

It was successful in saving his life, for instead of being sentenced to death the prisoner was sentenced to four years' imprisonment.

CHAPTER 15

# NATIVE RESERVE

In 1926, when the Sabi and Shingwedzi game reserves were united in the Kruger National Park, certain areas along the western boundary of the old Sabi Reserve were excised. In my own section, the Pretorius Kop area of the Park, much of the area excised, including part of the Sigaas River, was proclaimed a native reserve and at the time of its removal from the Park's territory it was literally packed with game. In fact, it is sad to relate that this portion covered some of our best game country as it was well watered and, with big *vleis* in most parts, there was always early summer grazing.

Needless to say, once the area was removed from the Park the game rapidly began to disappear, as natives and game do not make congenial neighbours. There was no longer any adequate means of protecting the game once outside our sphere of control, as the nearest police establishment was at White River – some thirty miles away – where there was only a sergeant and a trooper.

A pitiful situation arose almost immediately, as the natives, never slow to exploit such an opportunity, flocked in from every-

where and shooting and hunting with big packs of dogs was done quite openly. Many times while patrolling along my new boundary I saw what was taking place, but I was powerless to stop it although it hurt me very much to see my precious game, which for so many years I had guarded and cherished, rapidly being slaughtered off before my eyes with every fiendish method adopted by natives who are completely callous to animal suffering in their insatiable lust for meat.

This state of affairs continued for about three years and during this period I estimate that there must have been about three thousand head of game killed – including the less common types, such as roan and sable antelopes and reedbuck. In addition to the havoc wrought among the wretched animals by the natives in the newly-proclaimed native reserve, Europeans used to come down with wagons under the pretext of carting manure from the native kraals to be sold to the citrus growers at White River, but I doubt whether any wagon returned up the hill and to Legogote without two or three dead buck concealed beneath its buck-sail!

Finally, Colonel Stevenson-Hamilton, the warden of the Park, succeeded – after a lot of trouble on his part – in getting the policing of the native reserve vested in the Park, and I was allowed to patrol it with my native rangers.

A remnant of the game still remained there and we caught quite a lot of natives with firearms and also large packs of dogs, most of which were unlicensed. The latter I always destroyed as they were miserable, hungry, half-starved and neglected creatures. The poachers were sent to the warden's court at Skukuza, where they were tried. These measures considerably improved the poaching situation, although, of course, a certain amount is sure to continue in the native reserve.

On the first occasion on which I entered the native reserve after we had taken over its policing, we found where three sable antelopes had been shot when they came to drink in the Sigaas; and as this had only happened during the previous day we were able to follow the spoor of the hunters. This finally led us to a kraal about eight miles away where we found the meat in a hut. We arrested the owner of the hut who, of course, denied all participation in the shooting. Eventually, however, he handed over to me his rifle — a rusty old .303 — and half a dozen cartridges.

It was now about sundown and we still had eight miles to travel before reaching camp. Fortunately it was a bright moonlight night and while we were on our way we suddenly heard dogs barking. Hastening in the direction indicated by the increasing outcry we presently came up with several natives in the act of killing a waterbuck, which they had brought to bay in a pool in the Sigaas River. Of course, as soon as the natives observed me they bolted, but we caught one of the party who told us who the remainder were, and they were later arrested. It was just before midnight when we finally reached my small camp, and very hungry and tired we all were, and I had had nothing to eat since breakfast that morning.

Early on the following morning we heard a shot at no great distance and while proceeding in that direction we found a big waterbuck bull lying dead. There were no natives to be seen, so we proceeded to the nearest kraal, about half a mile away, and questioned its owner. As usual he "had not heard the shot" (it is really surprising how deaf natives are on certain occasions – the very reverse on others) and he earnestly assured me of his complete ignorance of the whole matter. However, it was quite plain to me that he was lying, and after being handcuffed he admitted having himself shot the waterbuck and unwillingly produced his rifle, stating that the bullet he used was the last he had – which might or might not have been true.

On that particular trip we discovered where eight head of game had been killed, and in the majority of the cases we caught the offenders. I managed to thin out considerably the amount of rifles being used, but there are still a few left. The natives manage, somehow, to acquire them from so-called white men who live near the boundaries of the Park.

I have also caught white poachers on several occasions, and naturally they waxed very sore about being arrested and fined; and some of them actually started a movement among the natives who had also been arrested and fined for poaching. These ingen-

ious and pleasantly disposed gentry informed the natives that if the latter helped to make a case against me by giving false evidence the result would be my discharge and, in that happy event, one of their white fellow conspirators would be put in my place, and after that everybody would be able to hunt as much as they liked! I heard  about this movement, but for a time took little notice of it as I did not anticipate that anything would come of it. However, in this I was proved to be unduly optimistic.

The aggrieved parties continued their operations among similarly disposed natives until they had collected enough false statements to enable them to work up a case against me, which they then handed over to the police. I suddenly found myself arrested and was taken to Barberton to appear before the magistrate. Naturally I engaged a solicitor and was let out on bail.

The case was remanded for Circuit Court and in the meantime I was suspended from my duties and another appointed in my place by the acting warden, Major Fraser. On the surface things did not look too good for me just then as, according to the native statements, I was accused of practically every sort of crime short of murder! However, I am happy to relate that when the case was brought before the Circuit Court the trial lasted three days, after which the jury, without retiring, returned a verdict of "not guilty" on all charges, so I was reinstated.

Some years after this somebody reported to the police commandant that every native in the reserve owned a rifle, so a big raid was carried out by the police. I think about one hundred white and black personnel must have been involved. One company started from the south – that is, from the Crocodile River – and the other half operated from the Sabi, the plan being that both

parties should spread out and thoroughly search each kraal and hut until they finally converged.

I was asked to assist with my rangers from my side and Ranger James to do so from his. Although I felt dubious about the results – as natives are not accustomed to keep such illegal possessions as rifles in their kraals – I naturally complied with the request. The operations lasted for two days and the net result was the finding of one ancient Martini rifle, which was triumphantly handed in at headquarters by the commandant and his men.

I think that most of the tourists who visit the Kruger National Park must obtain quite a lot of amusement through watching the troops of baboons that are plentiful throughout the sanctuary, especially in the vicinity of Pretorius Kop. They are amazingly human in their antics and the old male baboon always guards his troop. I have often watched one of these seniors run back and rescue a youngster left behind while the remainder of the troop were running away from supposed danger.

There is a kopje called Manunge[18] about a mile from Pretorius Kop rest camp, and this is a favourite sleeping place of the troop of baboons that inhabit this area. There is a big fissure in the steep rock face of this kop where they all sleep, perfectly secure in the knowledge that no leopard or lion could scale such a steep rock

---

[18] Manungu

in order to get at them. The other side of the kopje is equally inaccessible as there is a big flat rock, above which are some loose boulders. I have, on more than one occasion, seen lions on the top side of this flat rock, and baboons, approaching from the lower side, actually advance to within two or three yards of the lions, barking defiantly and grimacing at them – some bolder spirits even venturing almost close enough to pull the nearest lion's tail!

The remarkable degree of calculating intelligence of the baboon is well illustrated by such behaviour, for the animals are well aware that so long as they keep to the lower side of the rock, well below the lions, they are perfectly safe – no matter how infuriated the formidable objects of their impudence may become. If a lion was so misguided as to make a jump downwards at them, it would be hurled to pieces while falling down the rock.

The lions also being possessed of a good degree of intelligence, such episodes usually end with the great tawny cats retreating with as much display of haughty dignity as they can muster in the aggravating circumstances. A friend of mine actually managed to secure a cine picture of such a scene, and although I never saw the result he informed me that it was quite successful.

The families of our native rangers have a difficult time guarding their crops from raiding baboons; in fact during the period immediately previous to reaping the natives have to camp out in their lands. Some of the more aggressive and insolent "old men" baboons defy the women and will only submit to being chased away when a man appears on the scene. They seem capable of discriminating between men and women.

One of these old male baboons, as he stalks solemnly along through the veld, cunningly seeking out edible roots, bush fruits, scorpions, spiders and other dainties, with his immensely powerful, muscular body set off by the pompous, swaggering swing of his drooping tail, cuts what one might respectfully describe as a "fine figure of an ape"; and such old males are rightly treated with respect by even leopards and lions. Their physical strength is enormous, their great canine teeth as large as, or larger than, those of a leopard and their tempers short — as the terrified squeals of chastised youngsters at bedtime indicate, for these husky old fellows are great family disciplinarians!

During the old days, when we used to hunt lions in the reserve, on several occasions I located these beasts by following in the direction where baboons were barking. In one such instance I found two lions sitting under a tree in which an old man baboon had sought refuge from them. The distracted old boy was barking and grimacing at them all the time, and neither he nor the lions noticed my approach (it is indeed seldom that one can escape the vigilant eyes of a baboon in a tree). I shot both the lions, and the old baboon jumped out of the tree and made off as fast as he could, glancing in grinning anxiety over his shoulder from time to time to see, I suppose, whether the lions were after him.

These old male baboons are great fighters and their formidable teeth are as sharp as knives. Although my dogs have on occasion caught and killed them, they have also accounted for many dogs. When it seizes hold of a dog, a baboon first grabs a good mouthful of the unfortunate victim and then it pushes the animal away with both hands, meantime still holding on firmly with its teeth; thereby ripping the dog to pieces.

Fortunately wounds made by baboons do not seem to be poisonous and I have often sewn up nasty gashes caused by these animals with the surgical needle and a couple of hairs out of my horse's tail. The wounds have always healed quite easily, unless a big artery has been severed. In that case, of course, the dog soon bleeds to death as in the veld one does not carry artery forceps and surgical instruments. Oddly enough, I believe that a bite from a baboon kept in captivity invariably turns septic.

Talking of the tourists in the Kruger National Park reminds me that in the early days of the Park numbers of overseas tourists used to visit it, usually being brought in by taxis which were hired for the purpose. Of course, they were all especially keen to see lions and some of them used to promise the drivers of the cars (who were mostly men from local villages) half a crown for each lion spotted for them.

This rapidly proved a most profitable business for some of the drivers, who were clever lads. After encountering a pride say of six lions, the driver of the taxi would drive the party a few miles round and then bring them back to the same lot by another road.

Probably by this time the original pride had been joined by one or two more lions and thus the tariff increased, but in any case the visitors were usually none the wiser and quite reckless in their enthusiasm. Very often by the end of the trip the driver was richer by quite a few pounds.

Many visitors to the Park obtain much entertainment from the little grey vervet monkeys that will sit in the trees quite close to the road, watching the passing cars. If caught young, these monkeys make quite amusing pets. One day, while I was riding through the veld accompanied by my dogs, the latter chased a troop of vervets, which immediately made for and scaled the nearest trees. One poor little fellow, however, who could not have been more than a week old, fell off his mother's back and we found him hiding in the long grass. I dismounted and picked up the wizened grey mite, who clung confidently and tenaciously to my shirt front all the way home. I fed him on milk and he became most attached to me, following me faithfully around my camp.

Later I obtained a little mate for him – this time a female – but the escapades of those two soon taught me the full meaning of the expression "monkey tricks". Later on I could not allow them in my house, but one morning, while I was eating my breakfast, the male monkey sat watching me at the open window of the hut. Now, in those far-away bachelor days I was wont to time the boiling of my eggs by my pocket watch, which I would lay on the table in front of me while eating my porridge.

The monkey suddenly made one leap from the window, landed on the table, grabbed my watch, and was out through the window before I was fully aware of what had happened. In the next instant he was up a tree with the watch in his hand! I tried every method of persuasion, gentle and otherwise, to entice him to come down, but all to no purpose. Later in the day be grew tired of his new possession and dropped it, and of course that was the end of my watch.

On another occasion he stole a small kitten from the litter while their mother was away and away up the tree he went with the poor little mewing wretch, clutching it tightly to his breast and trying to nurse it. Again I tried every conceivable method to get him down, and again with no success, but this ended in a more tragic way as the monkey would not let go the kitten which, as it was still very small, finally died of starvation. He treated the dead kitten with the same finality as he had my watch – he dropped it.

When, however, he absconded with a tiny pup from a litter of fox terriers I thought it was time to chain him up – but how to

catch him now was a problem. I solved this by placing some mangoes, of which he was very fond, in one of my store huts, leaving the window open. As soon as I had concealed myself nearby he went in after the mangoes, whereupon I shut the window and so caught him – much to his annoyance, for he bit me severely in the arm.

He now suffered the almost unbearable indignity of having a strap tied round his waist and being chained to a tree until the pups had grown up – a matter of about two months – when he was again released. However, sad to relate, he finally came to a sticky end, being killed by one of my dogs which, I suppose, he had been teasing too much.

One obtains quite a lot of fun from some of the tourists who visit the Park. Once I was driving along in my car when I observed a stationary motor car in the road ahead. As I approached I saw two young girls seated in it while their companion, a young lad, was engaged in walking slowly towards some lions which were lying on a flat rock.

The girls seemed thoroughly frightened and repeatedly shouted to him to come back before the lions caught him, but the reckless young idiot, evidently intending to show off, took no notice and continued to advance. I quietly walked after him and he remained ignorant of my arrival until I asked him what he thought he was doing, and demanded his name and address.

At the unexpected sound of my voice he received such a fright that he could only gape at me, words seeming to fail him. Having obtained his address and car number, I admonished him for his foolish behaviour and lack of responsibility towards his companions, and informed him that I would have to report him to the police for breaking the Park's regulations by getting out of his car and walking towards lions (or any other game).

Another day I came on two cars that had turned off the road towards some lions – evidently to obtain a better view of the beasts, though they could see them quite plainly from the road. Getting out of my car, I walked up to them and very civilly informed them that they had broken the regulations and that it was my unpleasant duty to take their names and addresses and report them to the authorities.

One man replied, "How dare you speak to me in that manner, and what authority have you to take my name and address?" I informed him that I was a ranger, but he demanded to see my authority so I pointed to the badge on my shirt, and this finally appeared to satisfy him. I then asked the driver of the other car whether he also desired to see my badge, but his wife, who was sitting beside him, replied, "Oh no! You look the part!" And to this day I have not decided whether that was intended as a compliment or mere sarcasm!

On another occasion I came on to four young lads off the road proceeding towards some wildebeest grazing close by. Again I went through the usual procedure. I could see that they were out for a good time and they seemed to be quite jolly, having had a few drinks each. They accepted my authority in good part and asked me how much they would be fined. "Perhaps three or four pounds," I said, and at this the owner of the car (at least he was at the wheel) muttered, "Oh, Lad, we'll have to sell the old car!"

One dear old lady asked me innocently whether wildebeest ate the smaller buck, so I replied, "Madam, they eat grass!" She then said, "But the giraffes eat wildebeest, don't they?" and when I corrected her and told her that the giraffe browse off the leaves of the trees, she expressed her pleasure that they didn't all eat each other!

Sometimes people become very indignant when asked for their names and addresses and being told that they are guilty of breaking the rules of the National Park; occasionally they refuse to provide the necessary information. It was always a rule of mine never to argue with a tourist, and I can honestly say that I have never had any trouble. In such refractory cases I simply noted the number of the car and later obtained their names and addresses from the permit issued at the gate by which they entered the Park.

I dislike playing practical jokes on people as a rule, especially my native followers, as such pranks are apt to lessen their respect for one; but on one occasion I was unable to resist the temptation. I was out with a new native ranger who was rather inexperienced and a bit raw. As we were going along a big warthog boar came trotting past us, with his tail stiffly erect as usual. The two dogs I had with me were young and had not yet learnt completely that they were not to chase game, so they made off after the pig before I could stop them.

A little later I heard them barking and I knew then that they had either bayed up the warthog or had chased him into a hole. Following the sounds, I soon found the dogs standing round the entrance of an old antbear's hole at the foot of a big white ant hill. I knew that the pig was inside the hole, and it occurred to me that this was an excellent opportunity to teach my new ranger a little veldcraft.

First I caught the dogs and tied them to the trunk of a tree nearby. I then told the native to stand in front of the hole and to observe what would happen when I stood on the top side of the hole. I then, having taken up my position, gave a couple of heavy stamps with my boot and immediately out bolted the pig! It has been my experience when a warthog has thus gone to ground and the hole is not too deep, if you stamp with your foot a few times on the top side of the hole he will rush out, as they always back into the hole tail first.

In this case, as I expected, out came the pig; and as the man was standing right in front of the hole and it couldn't get past, in its haste it knocked his legs from under him, sending him flying, and soon disappeared. I knew that it could not hurt the man if it hit him head-on, as a warthog must always hold his head to one side before he can use his fighting tusks.

The man now picked himself up and, looking decidedly foolish, he remarked to me that he thought he was dead that time. I

replied, "Now you know not to stand in front of a warthog's hole when somebody stands above it!"

Warthog boars are great fighters and I have more than once noticed two boars engaged in combat. They appear to push at each other, shoulder to shoulder, all the time watching for an opportunity to get a cut in with the lower fighting tusks, which are sharp as razors from being constantly worn up against the big, curved upper digging tusks. When one of the contestants finds that he is getting the worst of it, he suddenly spins round and makes a bolt for it, pursued by his triumphant adversary. I have never been able to witness the end of such a fight as they always disappear in the bush, but I have seen the loser get badly gashed as he spins round to flee.

The bull sable antelope, too, is a great fighter. I once had an opportunity of watching two sable bulls going at it in real earnest; in fact, although I had approached to no great distance from them they were so fully engaged with each other that they took no notice of me. Sometimes they clashed their heads together, pushing each other, shoulder to shoulder; each carefully awaiting an opportunity to pierce his adversary with a vicious thrust of the rapier-like curved and massive horns.

Both contestants had got in a few digs, though not yet a serious one, as the skin and flesh was cut open and bleeding here and there. Finally one of them evidently decided that he had enough and he made a bolt for it with his victorious opponent in hot pursuit, and very soon they both vanished from my view.

I have more than once come across the remains of a sable which had been killed in a fight with another bull. Even lions are occasionally killed by sable, as the long and backwardly-curved horns can be swept back over practically the whole of their bodies, and when a lion jumps on to a big sable bull he takes a considerable risk – though I know that quite a number of sable antelopes are killed by lions.

CHAPTER 16

# BIRDS

The honeyguide is a little brown bird about the size of a sparrow. When it has located a bee hive it endeavours by incessant twittering to attract the attention of the first human being that happens to come along. Having done so, it makes short flights in the direction of the hive, perching on a branch from time to time to allow the follower to come up, and so on until the hive has been reached.

It then perches on the nearest tree and, gazing fixedly at the hive, remains quietly waiting for the reward, which usually takes the form of a piece of honeycomb or some bees' grubs left in the ground. Having thus been rewarded, the honeyguide may then lead its follower to another hive it happens to know about. I may say that in South Africa bees generally build in the hollow of a tree, and the usual native custom is to attack the nest with a few bunches of lighted grass and smoke the insects out, regardless of stings.

One day, when far away in the veld and short of food, I heard a honeyguide twittering very persistently, and determined to follow. I had always found these birds honest guides in spite of the stories about them sometimes leading on to a lion or a mamba; stories which in my own experience are entirely incorrect. Anyhow, I followed the one in question for a considerable distance and while doing so passed through a patch of thick scrub, which happened to conceal a quantity of what are known as "hellfire beans".

This bean grows on a creeper and when ripe the pods are of a beautiful golden colour and of velvety texture, but are covered with minute thorns, so small that the human eye cannot see them. When the plant is shaken or disturbed these thorns come off in a cloud, and woe betide the creature on whom they settle. At first they are not felt as they stick in the clothes, but after a while they work their way through and start a maddening irritation of the skin, on which they raise big blisters.

The only cure I know of is to strip off the clothes and rub the body all over with oil fat, but when miles from camp, agonies are suffered before anything can be done. I have seen natives who have come into contact with these beans make a fire and almost stand in it while burning themselves with a handful of lighted grass. They say this stops the irritation, but I never tried it myself.

On the occasion mentioned above the honeyguide conducted me ultimately to the hive, and it was only half an hour later that I felt the irritation and realised that I had gone through some "hellfire beans". Leaving my natives to follow, I mounted my horse and rode as hard as I could back to my camp, where I at once stripped off my clothes and rubbed myself with oil. However, the fresh trouble was that I had no other clothes to change into, so I had to go without any while the old ones were washed, shaken out and dried, as I was a long way from my main camp. Still, the washing did seem to have got rid of most of the thorns, when I was able again to dress!

Another interesting bird is known as the tick-bird or oxpecker. It lives on ticks, which it finds on game and domestic stock. It serves a most useful purpose, but sometimes when the tick has left  a sore it will keep picking away at that and make a nasty wound, which may get flyblown and full of maggots. This happens most frequently with donkeys. In the early days at M'timba before East Coast Fever attacked the cattle and compulsory dipping was instituted, there were always a number of these birds in the cattle kraal every morning running about on the bodies of the beasts and under their bellies, picking off the ticks, at that time very numerous.

Then came the dipping tanks in which cattle had to be immersed twice a week in an arsenical compound. This destroyed the ticks, but the tick-birds went on eating them afterwards just the same, and as they were impregnated with arsenic, the birds died. For many years I never saw any more tick-birds.

Recently a few have come in from areas where there is no dipping, but ticks are less numerous now and tick-birds may have become immune to arsenic to some extent; at all events one no longer finds dead ones lying about. In the Kruger National Park they are still to be seen in great numbers doing their work in keeping the game free from ticks.

The so-called *toppie* is also a useful little bird. It will always disclose the presence of a snake concealed in a bush or tree. These birds usually collect in small lots of from two to six and keep up an incessant chatter near the spot where the snake hides, and so if one searches closely one is likely to find it lying along or under a branch. Guided by the *toppies* I have shot many snakes about the camp.

Vultures, as everyone knows, are the scavengers of the veld, and any dead beast which has missed the eye of the carnivores is soon found and eaten. They are always in the sky but so high as not to be seen by the human eye, but should anyone of them see a dead beast on the ground and come towards it, he is soon seen by the others, who follow him.

Once, when travelling by lorry from Skukuza with

some natives riding on the back, we saw some vultures dropping like stones out of the sky about 50 yards off.

The men, knowing there was meat, asked my permission to go and look. I told them to hurry if they expected to find anything. I saw the vultures rising in clouds when the men approached and very soon the latter came with the remains of an impala which the vultures had just started on. Two men were carrying it on their shoulders and I saw the vultures swoop down several times in an attempt to regain their meat, rather an unusual occurrence, but no doubt they were very hungry. The men made for the lorry as fast as they could and the vultures flew off.

The giant bustard, which is very numerous in some parts of the Kruger National Park, is one of our largest game birds, often to be seen strutting about the veld in a very stately manner. In the breeding season the cock bird, when showing off, swells out his neck to about three times its normal size – enough to inspire anyone, even a bustard hen!

They are very good eating indeed. I have always pot-boiled them first and then poured off the first water as they have rather a rank flavour. When properly cooked, however, the slices off the breast are very tasty. These giant bustards live on lizards and insects and I once saw one devouring a chameleon. This, though, is no worse than the fowls that are allowed to roam round the yard looking for their food.

The yellow-billed and red-billed hornbills are very numerous throughout the Park. In Afrikaans these birds are known as *boskraaie*, and by the local natives they are called *kotokoto* – the sound of which greatly resembles the bird's call. In the nesting season the hen makes her nest in the bowl of a hollow tree. She remains within, shedding all her feathers and lining the nest with them. The male, meanwhile, plasters up the opening from the outside, leaving only a very narrow space through which to insert his bill in order to feed the incarcerated hen. The latter remains a prisoner until the chicks are big enough to leave the nest, when the plaster is broken open and the family liberated.

The helmet shrike can be seen in the more bushy areas. Travelling restlessly about in parties of from six to eight or more, they leisurely make their way through the bush, picking up any insects that may be around. Very attractive they look, as their black and white plumage imparts a flickering, rather butterfly-like effect. A native superstition in connection with these birds is that when they flit across the path of a traveller, the latter is in luck as he will be well received and given plenty to eat and drink when he reaches his destination.

The grey lourie, too, is encountered in most areas as he flops clumsily about the trees and bushes, looking for any wild fruits

or berries. This bird is more commonly known as the go-away bird, owing to its distinct cry of "Go away!" In the early days, when I used to do a bit of hunting, this bird proved to be most irritating as just as one was stalking up to some animal, the wretched bird would come and sit near one – commanding in no uncertain terms to "go away" – and of course the game at once knew that something was about and would clear.

Not so common is the secretary bird, usually to be seen strutting sedately about the veld, looking for insects, lizards and snakes, which they appear to relish. During the nesting season they can often be seen perched on top of one of the thorny mimosa trees where they build their nests, to which they return year after year.

I once climbed one of these trees and found two eggs in the nest. One of these I took home with me and placed under a broody hen. In due course the chick hatched and grew up, and it became quite a figure about the yard. I brought him up on small bits of meat until he was old enough to wander around and fend for himself on the mice and lizards that abounded in the yard.

I often watched him, when he was fully grown, walk round one of the dogs which would be lying asleep quite peacefully. Doiya, as he was called (that being the native name for a secretary bird), would then give the innocent dog a terrific kick, which would send it off yelping. Doiya would then strut off in the opposite direction, looking most innocent. This would certainly seem to suggest that a secretary bird is possessed of a sense of humour – albeit a warped one!

In course of time Doiya met his fate when one of the dogs got hold of him and bit him so badly that I had to destroy him. Such is usually the fate of tyrants! Unfortunately, it is also often the end of most wild pets.

CHAPTER 17

# HORSES

All my life I have loved a good dog and a good horse. I have devoted some space to the various dogs which I owned at one time or another, but I must say I was just as fond of my horses as I was of my dogs, and I can look back with great happiness to the good times spent with them, as well as with sorrow to their inevitable passing away. It is a tragedy that the lives of animals should be so relatively short.

Before the advent of the motor car and the construction of a certain number of roads throughout the Kruger National Park, the main means of transport for a ranger was his horse. If he was fortunate enough to possess two he considered himself very lucky indeed. Sometimes his horse made all the difference between life and death, since he lived far from civilisation and when injured or taken sick in the veld his horse was the only means of his getting home. I was very fond of my horses, and although I worked them hard (they were under the saddle almost daily) I always took great care of them.

Among the many horses I possessed at different periods of my career was a part Arab mare, Merrie. With a milk-white coat she carried black hoofs as tough as steel, and in all the many years I rode her unshod, often over exceedingly rough and stony country, she was never once footsore. In fact, never in her life did she require shoeing.

I bought her from a friend who, but for the fact that he was leaving South Africa for overseas, would never have parted with her. She was what was then known as "salted"; that is, she had contracted and recovered from the terrible scourge of horse sickness. Those were before the days when the system of inoculation against the disease had been discovered and put in practice, and as recoveries were in the ratio of only two or three per cent, salted horses were correspondingly valuable. Some of these animals used to have a slight relapse once a year, but if given complete rest for a week they would become quite fit again.

I had often seen my friend ride this mare, and also accompanied him when he was doing so, and had always coveted her; in fact had told him that if he ever thought of selling her I would like first refusal. Consequently, when she did become mine, I was a proud man. She had the heart of a lion, was as pretty as a picture and as good as she looked. No journey was too long for her – indeed, she

could usually outlast her rider. One day I rode her for 80 miles, and she was as fresh at the end as when she started. She would take anything I put her at, whether a deep donga, a fallen tree, a river or a spruit in flood. Moreover she was as tame as a lamb and a perfect shooting horse; I could fire from her back and she had not the slightest fear of lions or anything else. Needless to say, I took the greatest care of her; much more, indeed, than at that time I did of myself!

But paragon as she was, she did have one fault, which I never could explain and which happened only occasionally, once in about every three months and always at M'timba, where she was more highly fed and better stabled than when on patrol, though even then I always saw that she had the best I could give and was properly rugged up at night.

Sometimes I was prepared for these fits of cussedness and sometimes they caught me unawares. This was what usually happened. I would mount and she would go gently for perhaps 100 yards, then she suddenly would toss up her head violently. If I was prepared I would let the reins go quite slack so as not to jerk her mouth. She would repeat the performance two or three times and, if met with no opposition, would go on quietly for the rest of the day, but if I was caught unprepared, or my attention momentarily diverted, and thus allowed the bit to jerk her mouth as she tossed her head, then the fat was in the fire.

It appeared in fact to be just what she had been hoping for, and she would dance and prance round in circles, performing all kinds of circus tricks and go everywhere except the way I wanted her to go. The best, in fact, the only solution, I found, was to dismount and lead her for a quarter of a mile or so, and when remounting to be careful to have a quite slack rein. If this programme was adopted she would give no further trouble.

One day, however, I thought I would try to cure her by galloping her up and down a newly ploughed field. I cannot remember how many times we did it, I only know that she seemed to enjoy it more than I did and that when I wanted to stop and leave the field she insisted on continuing the exercise. So in the end I had to get off and lead her out.

Another time during her tantrums we happened to be close to a koppie several hundred feet high, covered with large boulders, flat rocks and bush. It was so steep that it used to take me all my time to climb up on foot. Thinking I might thus stop her nonsense I put her at the koppie, which she at once went up like a bird right to the top, much to my discomfort, as I was constantly in imminent danger of slipping off backwards over her quarters. It was a feat which I am sure no animals except baboons and klipspringers had ever accomplished before.

On arrival at the summit she appeared anxious to run down the other side, but that would have been risking both our necks and I could not in any case have ridden down either by that route or by the one we came up without falling over her ears! So I gave best, dismounted and led her down. On arriving at the foot she looked up and whinnied, as much as to say, "We did it!"

Suffice it to say I never succeeded in breaking her of her queer fits of temper, and eventually when she became old I pensioned her off.

I had one foal from her, which I named Sultan. He was by a

grey stallion belonging to Colonel Stevenson-Hamilton which was also part Arab. When about two years old the colt developed horse sickness and nearly died, and though with careful nursing I pulled him round, his legs remained swollen for a long time and eventually one fetlock remained so permanently thick that I found him useless for my work and had to sell him.

Another old favourite was named Dandy and he was one of the first horses that the Veterinary Department gave out to farmers in horse sickness areas as being immunised against horse sickness. I sent two of my men to collect him at the Nelspruit railway station, and when they arrived back at my camp with the horse everybody turned out to see him, as the acquisition of a new horse was a great and important local event in those days.

The new arrival was hardly an inspiring sight as we first saw him; I believe that he had just been running wild in the camp at Pretoria for some time past and apparently had never been stabled, fed or groomed during that pleasant period of his existence. I even heard one of my men mutter, sarcastically enough for a native, "He's got a nice long tail!" At any rate I immediately set to work to improve matters, brushing, grooming and feeding him, and in a month's time he looked a very different animal.

I rode Dandy for thousands of miles; he turned out to be an excellent shooting pony and he never once let me down. With him I shot many lions in the old days – unlike most horses he was not afraid of them. Several times I took him up to a dead lion which I had shot and he showed no fear of it, occasionally even giving it a nip with his teeth. He also seemed quite unresentful of having fresh lion skins packed on his back.

Dandy was a most useful shooting horse and I could always fire quite confidently from his back. He seemed to enjoy shooting and always to sense when I was out to kill a buck for meat for the camp. This was of great value to me, since during the summer months the grass was very long and one was unable to see a reedbuck unless one was sitting on a horse. I had the impression that he tried to hold his breath so as not to disturb my aim when I was about to fire from his back. When I had shot the buck and covered it up against the vultures, I would often leave the reins lying slack on Dandy's neck and he would proceed straight back to camp. Having collected men to come and carry the meat, I would get into the saddle again and Dandy would bring me straight back to the spot.

This reminds me of an amusing incident. I had gone out one day to shoot a reedbuck for meat (these antelopes were very plentiful near my place at that time), but the grass was very long and we were unable to locate any for some time. Presently we saw a donkey feeding some way off across the spruit. Dandy evidently came to the conclusion that here, at last, was one of those damned, elusive reedbuck, for he firmly insisted on advancing in the donkey's direction. I repeatedly tried to turn him, but he stubbornly persisted, and in the end I thought it was best to let him go and find out his mistake for himself. When we got near enough for Dandy to take a good look at the donkey, I could almost fancy the expression of disgust on his equine face as he turned right round in the opposite direction and carried me away!

Dandy was also clever at opening the tap of the water tank

with his teeth when he wanted a drink. Unfortunately, though, he was unable to close it again and thus a lot of water was wasted every time he felt thirsty. Water was a very precious commodity since we had to depend on two tanks for our supply, otherwise it had to be carried in barrels on a wagon for the distance of a mile. I was therefore forced to put a lock on the tap.

Dandy was passionately fond of mangoes, of which there were several trees growing in the yard. He would help himself from the branches and later on in the season, when there were no more within reach, he would back up against the tree and bump up against it with his hindquarters, thereby shaking the ripe fruit on to the ground. He was adept, also, at opening the yard gate, when he would go careering across the veld until the men brought him back. During the cold nights out camping he loved to warm himself by the campfire.

I rode poor old Dandy for twenty-one years, and then, as his age was telling on him and he became a victim to rheumatism and found no more joy in life, I sent him to the Happy Grazing Grounds; and there I hope one day to see him again with all my other animal friends.

His successor was Patch –

also a good shooting horse, though not so sound as Dandy. After many years of hard work he also grew old and was pensioned off, as by that time immunised horses were easy to obtain. While away in the veld I was accustomed to leave old Patch in the charge of my men. Every evening he would come home by himself, and the men would feed him and lock him up for the night in the stable. And then, one evening, he did not come home, and by the time his absence was noticed it was too dark to go out and search for him. Next morning my men found that a lion had killed him about two hundred yards from the stable. They set a trap by his remains and caught the killer, and so old Patch's tragic end was avenged.

CHAPTER 18

# LIONS

And now, since lions are always popular fare with readers of books like this one of mine, let me end these reminiscences with just a few accounts of some more unusual adventures with them.

One Christmas morning, as I performed the first function of the day – that of visiting the stables to feed my horse – I found awaiting me a native from a neighbouring kraal. He complained that lions had killed two head of cattle and three donkeys at his kraal during the night, and begged me to go and hunt them.

There is no rest for a game ranger, even on Christmas Day! So I saddled my horse, called some of my native rangers and dogs, and set out for the scene of the disaster.

Having found the remains of the cattle and donkeys we took up the spoor of the lions, and this led into a thick patch of bush alongside a granite koppie due east of M'timba. I instructed the men to allow me about ten minutes in which to get into position where I could see the lions if they broke cover. A big rock, jutting out from the koppie, seemed ideal for my requirements and here

I took up my stance – leaving my horse about fifty yards away. He was a good horse and I knew that he would remain there until I returned to him. I then shouted to the men to drive the bush.

However, instead of breaking cover where I had anticipated their so doing, the lions passed up the hill behind me, in fact, within a few yards of where I was stationed. They came along so silently that, had it not been for the dislodgement of a few stones, they would probably have escaped my attention. As it was, hearing the clatter of falling stones, I glanced round in time to see a lion slinking past.

I instantly fired and hit him, and as he was on a steep slope he rolled down into the bush below. Then appeared another, which I also shot, and he too rolled down into the bush. Finally, a lioness appeared, but as she was exactly opposite me when I hit her she came tumbling down within ten yards of the rock on which I was standing and I can hardly say that I greeted her appearance, in such circumstances and at such close quarters, with the pleasant sentiments of goodwill usually associated with Christmas Day.

As the lioness lay roaring with rage and pain I pushed home the bolt of my rifle, but to my anxiety heard no cartridge being slipped forward into the breech. Desperately I pulled back the bolt – to find the magazine quite empty! To this day I cannot explain how this neglectful state of affairs occurred, as I was invariably most careful to have a full magazine before setting forth – perhaps on this occasion the fact that it was a time of festivity may have had something to do with it. Anyway, there I was, with an empty rifle and faced by a wounded lioness in a very dangerous frame of mind – still, fortunately, unaware of my presence so close to her.

I had a full packet of cartridges in the wallet of my saddle, but that was on my horse fifty yards away and my nearest route to this was blocked by the lioness. The only thing left for me to do was to remain as still as possible in the hope that she would not see me and that she would soon expire. I must point out that there was no way of escape from the rock, as the lioness barred the way on one side and on the other there was a drop of forty feet.

Eventually, to my very great relief, she toppled over dead, and I wasted no time in jumping over her dead body and running over to my horse, which was still feeding quietly where I had left him. Having refilled my magazine with cartridges from the packet in the saddlebag, I returned to my position on the rock.

After a while I heard the natives making a great deal of noise in the bush. The hubbub resounded from some distance and I was unable to make out what was going on. Eventually one of my policemen appeared on the opposite side of the kloof, and he informed me that two natives had been mauled pretty badly by one of the lions that had rolled down the slope previously after I had wounded them.

I followed him back and found one native rather badly bitten in the arm and the other on the thigh, and they were both bleeding profusely. In order to stop the bleeding they had stuffed the tooth holes with grass and leaves. Nearby lay a dead lion, and I subsequently learnt that these two men had not started on the hunt with us, but that, hearing about it, they had joined in later; their normal judgment no doubt slightly impaired by the fact that they had been celebrating Christmas at a neighbouring kraal and consequently were full of *skokiaan* and courage.

Approaching the sphere of operations on their own, it befell them, of course, to blunder upon the wounded lion in a patch of scrub at the lower end of the bush; and a wounded lion is loath to leave cover and go into the open. They tackled it with their assegais and the lion got hold of one, biting him badly in the arm. Then his pal went in with an axe and chopped the lion about the head, whereupon the lion let go his first adversary and attacked the newcomer, seizing him by the thigh. With commendable courage (I doubt whether the full effects of the *skokiaan* still persisted after the sobering effect of his recent mauling) the first man again came to the rescue, and this time he succeeded in finishing off the wounded lion with his assegai.

I knew that there was still one wounded lioness about and another unwounded one in the kloof, so, not wishing to leave these (especially the wounded one) in order to attend the injured

natives, I dispatched the latter, who assured me that they could walk with the aid of some companions to M'timba – which was distant about one mile – with instructions to my wife to attend temporarily to their wounds.

We then followed the two lions and finally I shot them both. By this time a large crowd of natives had joined us, attracted by the shooting and noise, and I induced them to carry the dead lions to M'timba, just as they were, slung along poles. The natives meanwhile were resting in the shade. The one with the bitten leg hobbled up to the carcass of the lion which had mauled him, knelt down beside it, and began to tear it with his teeth! I did not realise at the time that my wife, unaware that both casualties were full of native beer, had given each of them a stiff tot of brandy and aspirin, which possibly accounted for such odd behaviour.

I dressed their wounds thoroughly, and having rubbed the latter full of permanganate I dispatched the two heroes to Barberton Hospital, whence in about a month's time they returned – none the worse for their adventure.

One day, while I was out riding with only a fly whisk in my hand, as my horse rounded a small bush we came face to face with a big black-maned lion. I think he must have been fast asleep and so had failed to hear my horse's footsteps until we had arrived within a few yards of him. Had he been less deeply asleep he would have slunk away long before this. However, we were too close to him now so he just lay flat on his belly, growling very unpleasantly with his ears flattened angrily. Fortunately, the wind was in the right direction — that is, blowing from me to him — otherwise my pony would never have stood it, as all animals instinctively dread the smell of lion.

Though the pony could clearly see the lion and was becoming decidedly fidgety, I firmly compelled him to face it as I knew that if I turned and galloped away it would probably chase me. It was an awkward few moments before the lion evidently saw that we meant to stick it out (or perhaps he sensed that there was no immediate danger to himself), and he decided that his best course was to retreat.

I saw him turn his shaggy head, glancing covertly behind him to see that all was safe, and he then turned about and walked away in a crouching attitude until about twenty paces away before looking back to see whether we were still there. I then shouted at him and he broke into a trot, and then into a canter, and finally disappeared in the bush. This had just been a game of bluff, and I had won. Of course, this was evidently not a bad-tempered lion — had he been a less peacefully disposed one we might not have been let off so lightly!

That lions are notoriously unpredictable in behaviour I think the following incident will show.

I had gone out one morning to shoot a wildebeest for the gang of labourers engaged in repairing the road. In due course I sighted a solitary old bull (on such occasions we always try to pick solitary beasts so as to save younger animals and also to avoid alarming a herd) and, firing from the lorry in which I was riding, I dropped him in his tracks. I had brought a few men with me on the lorry to load the dead animal, but hardly had the

wildebeest collapsed when one of the men shouted, "Look at the lions!" and, sure enough, several of these animals had appeared out of the bush and were hastening rapidly towards the dead wildebeest. I then jokingly told the men to chase the lions away from their meat, a suggestion that was evidently not received with enthusiasm.

Intending to set a worthy example, I dismounted from the lorry and proceeded to walk towards the lions – of which there were now quite a number – thinking that they would beat a retreat, as they so often do when approached by man. However, in this case I was mistaken, as they simply crouched in the grass with flattened ears and switching tails, snarling and growling and looking very nasty indeed. Evidently they were very hungry and obviously quite prepared to dispute possession of that wildebeest.

Frankly, I didn't like it at all. The prospect of having to run back to the lorry with the laughing men all looking on, after having put up such a brave show, was not at all pleasing! Still, shooting lions was now forbidden in the Kruger Park except under exceptional circumstances, so feeling decidedly small I cautiously backed towards the lorry, holding my rifle ready.

I then jumped on to the lorry and instructed the driver to drive up to the wildebeest quickly, in order to get there before the lions. When we reached it we found one lion already crouched

upon the carcass, busily tearing away at it. How it had got there nobody noticed.

I again got off the lorry and began to shout at the lion, but it was very hungry and so indeed were all the others by their appearance, and they just remained growling very threateningly. There seemed nothing for it under the circumstances but to shoot the lion on the kill, and this I did. The men lost no time in loading the bodies of lion and wildebeest on the lorry – in fact I do not remember their having performed a job so quickly, before or since.

When we had all safely embarked once more we looked round and saw the other lions – some twenty of them – still coming on to where the wildebeest had fallen. The pride consisted mostly of young lions, about half-grown, in very poor condition. Why their condition was so bad is difficult to explain as there were plenty of wildebeest about. Perhaps it was just because they had been unfortunate in hunting lately. One dead buck would not have gone far among a crowd like that.

While on one of my patrols, trekking with wagon and oxen along the road now known as the Jock of the Bushveld road (it was formerly the old Delagoa Bay road of the transport riders in the early days), we were caught in a severe thunderstorm with rain pour-

ing down in torrents. We were soon thoroughly drenched, but we had to proceed to our outspan on the Mtomene Spruit. The first thing I did after making camp was to oil my rifle.

During the night a pride of lions tried to attack the oxen, but they were kept off by the dogs and by the men throwing fire-brands in their direction. The lions, however, obstinately renewed their attacks with the result that we were kept awake all night, but towards dawn, fortunately, they moved away. We had had no time the previous evening to make a scherm (the usual rough fence of thorny bushes), and the lions might easily have caught the oxen, which had merely been tied to their yokes.

The next morning broke fine and sunny so I followed the lions' spoor, which was easily noticeable in the wet ground from the rain of the evening before. The lions travelled for some miles before they lay down in the open, evidently for the purpose of sunning themselves. I managed to get very close before killing one lioness and wounding another, but not very badly, as she jumped up and, evidently not knowing whence the shot came, ran towards a nearby spruit and, incidentally, straight for myself. She did not see me as I was standing behind a very small bush, just large enough to conceal me from her view. As she came I pushed home the rifle bolt again, but to my annoyance could hear that the cartridge had not been pushed home in the breech. I tried several times but with the same result; although I was certain that there were still eight bullets in the magazine as I had left camp with a full magazine.

All this time the lioness was trotting straight towards me and when she got within five yards of where I stood – quite still, and devoutly hoping that she would pass me by – she saw me. I do not think she could quite make me out as I remained perfectly motionless, but she halted, staring straight at me, looking very cross and growling threateningly. I think that if I had then made

a movement she would have had me. For what seemed an eternity we remained thus; and then she suddenly trotted past, down towards the spruit.

It now flashed through my mind that the magazine was not in its right position, so I gave it a good rap with the palm of my hand and the resulting click satisfied me as to what had been the cause of the trouble. I quickly fired again and this time I killed the lioness. Afterwards, on thinking it all over, it struck me that when drying my rifle the previous evening I had not pushed the magazine home properly.

During the whole of the above episode my men had been standing like statues, not far behind me. I had not dared to turn my head to look, but I knew they were there. While we were skinning the two lions one old man exclaimed, "Nkosi, that lioness was nasty! If she had only kept her mouth shut it would not have been so bad, but when she growled close to me it made my inside turn!"

I will end this chapter with another instance of native superstition. Some years ago a certain pride of lions gave a lot of trouble among native kraals near M'timba; killing cattle, donkeys, pigs and even fowls. In fact they succeeded in killing nearly all the pigs; jumping into the sties and killing them there. Finally a large hunt was organised in which a number of the native stock owners joined.

While following the lions' spoor towards a big kloof on the side of a hill, where the lions used to lie up for the day, I saw one of the men, who was leading, break off the branch of a leafy shrub called by the natives m'telemba. It has a very soft wood and the leaves and branches are very limp and droopy. This branch he threw across the spoor of the lions and, in response to my question, he explained that the idea was to make the lions, whose spoor we were following, become limp like the branch.

A little further on, the same man went down on his knees and clasped his hands in front of him – all his companions doing likewise – offering up a prayer to the spirits of their ancestors to assist us to find the lions and kill them.

The spirits apparently took a favourable view of their requests, for in due course we came up with the lions and with luck I managed to shoot three of them, and the remainder departed from the district.

# POSTSCRIPT

Now, after forty-four years of service under my old chief, Colonel J. Stevenson-Hamilton, in the old game reserve and the Kruger National Park – and having been privileged to see it grow from what might be termed nothing, it is today the finest wildlife sanctuary in the world – I have handed on my work to my son, and I feel sure he will carry on from where I left off.

It was a hard life: full of risks; but we were compensated by the interesting things we saw and did.

# METRIC TABLE

| | | |
|---|---|---|
| 1 foot | = | 0.3048 m |
| 1 inch | = | 2.54 cm |
| 1 gallon | = | 4.546 litre |
| 1 mile | = | 1.609 km |
| 1 square mile | = | 2.589 sq. km |
| 1 square foot | = | 0.092 sq. m |
| 1 morgen | = | 2.116 acres |

# PLACE NAMES

| THEN | NOW |
|---|---|
| Eastern Transvaal | Mpumalanga, South Africa |
| Lourenço Marques | Maputo |
| Northern Transvaal | Limpopo, South Africa |
| Portuguese East Africa | Mozambique |
| Rhodesia | Zimbabwe |
| Transvaal | Gauteng, Mpumalanga, Limpopo and North-West provinces, South Africa |